BE THE DRAGON

9 Keys to Unlocking Your Magic

Catherine J. Manning

— ILLUSTRATED BY —

Melanie Demmer

WORKMAN PUBLISHING

NEW YORK

For Cara and Lilah, the fiercest and loveliest new dragonlings I know.
—C.J.M.

To my wisest and bravest friend, Millie.
—M.D.

Library of Congress Cataloging-in-Publication Data is available.

ISBN 978-1-5235-1141-9

Design by John Passineau
Illustrations by Melanie Demmer

Workman books are available at special discounts when purchased in bulk for premiums and sales promotions as well as for fundraising or educational use. Special editions or book excerpts can also be created to specification. For details, contact the Special Sales Director at specialmarkets@workman.com.

Workman Publishing Co., Inc.
225 Varick Street
New York, NY 10014-4381
workman.com

WORKMAN is a registered trademark of Workman Publishing Co., Inc.

Printed in China
First printing August 2021

10 9 8 7 6 5 4 3 2 1

CONTENTS

DRAGONS: AN INTRODUCTION

Dear Reader,

I'm sure you've heard all the hero stories. Knights charging into battle to save the kingdom. Princesses growing into queens—fair, noble, quick to lead. But have you ever considered that the heroes we need most are . . . dragons?

"Dragons?" you say.

"As the heroes?" you ask.

I know, I know. But dragons, you see, are brave and fearless creatures with fire in their bellies, wisdom in their eyes, feelings in their scales, and hearts so big that they will welcome into their world any weary traveler, lost soul, or human friend in need of a place to belong. That's how I, a former royal biographer, left the dark libraries and empty battlefields and grand ballrooms to become a dragon myself.

"*You became a dragon?*" you ask.

Yes.

You see, the first time I saw a dragon, I shrieked like a banshee and ran face-first into the wall. When I came to, the dragon—Beppalina was her name—had made a cozy nest of grass and ferns where I could rest. She'd tucked her tail securely around me to keep me warm. When she saw that I was awake, she began to roar.

I followed her to the edge of a cliff where she roared into the wind, tongue wagging in the breeze. She was listening to the sound of her own voice. I braced my boots on the rocky terrain. I took a deep breath. I roared into the wind, too. Beppalina laughed so hard, flames shot out of her nose. My roar didn't bellow, it didn't echo, it barely reached Beppalina's small ears some twenty feet above my head. But I felt my lungs rattle. My heart pounded. My toes gripped the rocky earth through my leather boots as I rooted myself to the ground. I roared again and again and again.

Beppalina joined in and we roared together—a fiery chorus from the top of the mountain, bellowing for all to hear. From that day on, Beppalina and I met each Wednesday to climb to the highest point and let out all our roars together. She introduced me to her friends (you'll meet them soon). I took flight lessons (don't look down!). And mud baths (self-care is most important).

That is how I started my quest to become a dragon. And now you can embark on the journey, too! Read on, dear reader, and follow the steps to become the dragon you really are. Anyone can do it!

Here's where you begin:

1. Share your magic.
2. Listen—to yourself and to others.
3. Be brave enough to take risks that will help you grow.
4. Believe in yourself.
5. Do what you love.
6. Take good care of yourself so you can take care of others.
7. Be the one and only YOU.
8. Follow your own unique path and don't compare yourself to others.
9. Stick with the dragons that make you glow and help you grow.

Dragons come in all shapes and stripes. We don't all have the same scales and tails. So don't worry if you think you don't look the part. There is magic in us all if you only dare to look.

In the pages that follow, you'll meet the dragons who helped me on my quest and hear about everything I learned as I made my own transformation. Dare to be brave enough to take your first flight. Unlock your unique powers to share with the world. Test your skills along the way. And in the end, you'll discover the dragon hero in you, too.

KNOW YOURSELF

Once you start down this path, there is no turning back. The time has come to find out who you'll be in the face of any challenge.

What type of dragon are you?

1 Where would you most like to live?

A. Near the ocean
B. On a mountain
C. In a forest
D. In the desert
E. On a savannah

2 What is the best feeling in the world?

A. Being fresh and clean after a bath
B. The wind on your snout
C. Grass tickling your hide
D. The sun warming your scales
E. Moonlight washing over you

3 You would describe yourself as:

A. Caring
B. Brave
C. Curious
D. Passionate
E. Calm

4 What do you dislike the most?

A. Heat
B. Crowds
C. Heights
D. Cold
E. Mornings

5 **What magical power sounds the coolest?**

A. Controlling the weather
B. Flying
C. Invisibility
D. Breathing fire
E. Night vision

6 **What is your best subject in school?**

A. Science
B. Art
C. Math
D. PE
E. English

7 **What sounds like the best way to spend an afternoon?**

A. Swimming
B. Getting into a snowball fight
C. Exploring
D. Going to the beach
E. Baking for your clan

8 **What is your biggest pet peeve?**

A. Someone tugging on your tail
B. Getting dirty
C. Being cooped up inside
D. Being told what to do
E. Not finishing a book or project

9 **What color would you paint your cave or grotto?**

A. Blue
B. White
C. Green
D. Red
E. Yellow

10 **How would you describe your clan?**

A. You have a lot of distant cousins.
B. You all tend to do your own thing.
C. You do your best bonding one-on-one and outside.
D. You have a lot of loud talkers.
E. You tend to eat dinner and dessert together.

QUIZ RESULTS

Mostly As:

You are a **WATER DRAGON**. Residing in oceans, rivers, lakes, and the occasional rain forest, water dragons are usually calm and thoughtful creatures. They love fish, music, and stormy weather (especially when they get to create it!). They dislike dry heat and having their tails tugged. Water dragons' powers include making it rain, healing, and breathing underwater.

Mostly Bs:

You are an **AIR DRAGON**. Mountaintops, cliffs, or other places with a high elevation are the places these dragons call home. They love cloud-watching, playing in the snow, and whistling. They are not fans of dirt or large crowds. Their powers often consist of becoming invisible (or cloaking), super speed, and blowing big gusts of wind.

Mostly Cs:

You are a **GROUND DRAGON**. These great beasts mostly live in caves, in forests, and on savannahs. Their interests include exploring, grass, and belly rubs. They will avoid scary stories and spiders. Ground dragons have super strength and camouflage capabilities, and are whizzes at charms.

Mostly Ds:

You are a **FIRE DRAGON**. Most often, these dragons live in deserts and on tropical islands because they love the heat. They also tend to like sports, sand, and cooking (particularly roasting and barbecuing). They do not enjoy the cold or being told what to do. Their powers include breathing fire, age shifting, and immunity.

Mostly Es:

You are a **MOON DRAGON**. These gentle giants live anywhere with a good view of the sky, particularly on savannahs and plains. They come out at night and love sweets, tie-dye, crystals, and a good story. They tend to dislike mornings and public speaking. Their powers include glowing, night vision, and future-telling.

#1
Share your magic.

CRACKING THE EGG

Thousands of years ago, the Earth was in chaos. It was still new, you see, and new things tend to need some time and care to sort themselves out. The seas boiled, mountains tumbled, and grass was shocked with ice. Creatures of all shapes and sizes—dragons, unicorns, elves, fairies, princesses, knights, and goblins—did not handle this chaos well. They fought about things like whose turn it was to straighten up the forest, or who got the last cherry blossom tree of the season, or who won the Goblin Games.

The fighting only caused more chaos. Not only did wind tear up the land and cascading rain cause massive floods, but fires sprung up from the Earth's very core. As the creatures took shelter, hoping it would stop, the stories began about the most incredible token—a giant egg perched on a mystical island in the middle of the unknown sea. Rumor had it that the egg contained special powers that would set the world right. But only those who already had these powers would be able to find it.

Soon creatures ventured out into the storm to search far and wide for the Great Egg. They listed all the magic they believed they shared with the egg: knights had super strength and speed; fairies could cast charms like no other; goblins could grimace so hard they'd shatter the egg with a look; elves were creative and cunning. However, none were able to find the island, let alone get close to the egg. The seekers returned home empty-handed. They started to believe that the egg was just another fairy tale, another story made up to entertain or to help one sleep at night.

Then one day, eight dragons flying about their normal business were pulled by the wind and arrived on the mystical island at the very same time. The Great Egg hummed, calling them to come closer. The dragons each placed a paw on the massive shell. *Crack!* The dragons were startled and pulled their paws back. After all this time of hearing about the egg, they didn't want to be the ones to break it. But the egg hummed louder, calling them back. Slowly, the dragons formed a protective circle around the egg and placed their paws gently back on its shell. *Crack! Crack! Crack!* Suddenly, the egg burst open, shooting sparks high into the sky! A golden piece of courage, a glimmering chip of wisdom, a dazzling bit of kindness, a flashing cut of passion, a gleaming portion of justice, a sparkling slice of confidence, a twinkling chunk of ambition, and a flickering hunk of empathy—the traits that the eight dragons themselves possessed. For, you see, this was the real magic of the egg, and these were the powers that would set everything right.

The sparkling insides soared across the world. Balance started to seep back into the Earth, allowing the oceans and the mountains and the grass to return to their normal tasks of making waves, standing tall, and being wonderfully green. Creatures everywhere stopped their squabbling to look at the beauty before them, the shiny power of the egg's insides reflected in the stars and seas and, most important, in one another. Now their greatest strengths shone just as brightly as the egg had. Many of the silly ongoing fights were resolved in that shared moment of wonder, and the creatures started to see not only what they had in common with one another, but they also began celebrating their glittering differences.

Meanwhile, the dragons returned to their lives and picked up right where they left off. You see, when you shine with courage, wisdom, kindness, passion, justice, confidence, ambition, and empathy, magic unites the world.

SIMILARITIES AND DIFFERENCES

It was only after the powers of the Great Egg were released that the creatures began recognizing the similarities they shared with one another—as well as celebrating their differences. Take a peek around. What other types of creatures do you relate to? The results might surprise you!

If you were not a dragon, what other mythical creature would you be?

1 **What would make up your perfect afternoon?**

A. Strolling through a sunlit forest
B. Soaring through the clouds
C. Tinkering with projects at home
D. Taking a nice swim

2 **Where would you most like to travel?**

A. A lake surrounded by mountains
B. A grand palace
C. A charming village
D. A tropical cove

3 **What is your favorite color?**

A. Purple
B. Red
C. Green
D. Blue

4 **What is your favorite type of celebration?**

A. A birthday
B. A coronation
C. A holiday
D. A festival

5 **If you had unlimited supplies, what would you create?**

A. A shawl made of morning dew
B. A golden trumpet
C. Shoes or toys
D. Shell jewelry

6 **What qualities do you look for in a friend?**

A. Sweetness
B. Loyalty
C. Intelligence
D. Fun-loving spirit

7 **What is your favorite season?**

A. Spring
B. Fall
C. Winter
D. Summer

8 **What is your ideal meal?**

A. A leafy salad
B. A roast, potatoes, and a decadent dessert
C. Cookies
D. Seaweed wrap

9 **Most of the time, I would say I am:**

A. Mellow
B. Stubborn
C. Inventive
D. Curious

10 **When in a tough situation, I:**

A. Wait to see what happens
B. Forge ahead
C. Find a friend to help
D. Depends on my mood

QUIZ RESULTS

Mostly As:

You are a **UNICORN**. While many stories suggest that unicorns are rare, this is, in fact, untrue. Unicorns are just very good at staying out of sight when they do not want to be found, most being a bit shy. However, their bonds with friends tend to be lifelong. They are smart, kind, and helpful. Unicorns can be found in woodsy areas and often have the powers of invisibility, especially when they feel overwhelmed in crowded areas, and healing, which comes from being sensitive and in tune with their environment. They love dandelions as a sweet treat.

Mostly Bs:

You are a **GRYPHON**. Half eagle, half lion, gryphons are regal creatures and many are born leaders. They speak out against injustices, and when used for good, their stubbornness can help make great change. They are often quite fond of cheese and like to scratch their talons against smooth bark (growing talon pains are the *worst*). They are expert fliers and take great pride in making their homes elegant and sophisticated.

Mostly Cs:

You are an **ELF**. Small and clever, elves are makers at heart. They take great pride in their craft of choice, which can range from making shoes to toys to cookies—or even unconventional items like power tools. Elves tend to like the company of others, which gives them more energy and joy. They live in large groups, lots of times in cozy cottages, which are often decorated with their favorite posters and brightly colored leaves.

Mostly Ds:

You are a **MER**. A mer has the tail of a fish and the body of a human. While we most often hear of the merfolk who live in the ocean, there are freshwater clans that reside in lakes and rivers as well. They tend to be free spirits who enjoy trying their fins at a variety of activities—from singing to seaweed-weaving to underwater gymnastics to coral architecture to collecting all types of rocks. Though they can be forgetful, they also share new facts and skills with their loved ones every day.

QUEST

Treasure Hunt for a Friend

POWER UNLOCKED: Kindness
BRAVERY RATING: 🔥🔥

Friendliness is one of the most powerful types of magic. Why not take this opportunity to reach out to a new friend and maybe even offer a small, thoughtful gift? By being welcoming and understanding of others, you may find new folks for your clan!

What you'll need:
- An outdoor area you can explore
- Paper (optional)
- Tape (optional)

STEP 1: Make a list of things that you can find near your abode that another creature might like. You can also use the list below as a guide, or create your own.

Unicorn: Dandelions for their dessert
Gryphon: Bark for their talons
Elf: Bright leaves for decorating

Mer: Unique rocks for collecting
Human: Any of the above. Or perhaps a flower, a pine cone, or a shell.

STEP 2: Head to an outdoor area and explore. See how many items on your list you can find. Select your favorites.

STEP 3: Tape the items to a piece of paper and write a little note. For example, *Dear Neighbor, I thought you might enjoy this bright and colorful flower. Your new friend, [sign your name]*

STEP 4: Leave the gift in a spot where your neighbor/new friend can find it.

QUEST

THE GREAT (CONFETTI) EGG

POWER UNLOCKED: Wisdom
BRAVERY RATING: 🔥🔥🔥

You've got a lot to offer under that shell. One of the wisest things a dragon can do is to recognize the magic in themselves and others, and share it with the world.

ASK AN ELDER DRAGON

What you'll need:

◆ **Raw egg(s)**
◆ **Food coloring**
◆ **Vinegar**
◆ **Water**
◆ **Confetti or brightly colored glitter or fairy dust. Choose colors and textures that reflect your very best traits. Are you full of** yellow **sunshine? Are you able to calm anyone down with your peaceful** blue **roars? Are you full of** red **zippy passion and fun?**
◆ **Tissue paper (various colors to match your food coloring)**
◆ **Glue stick**

STEP 1: Gently tap the top of your egg with the end of a spoon to create a small hole. (You can also ask an elder dragon to use a needle or screwdriver.) Shake out the contents until it is empty.

STEP 2: Mix 10 to 20 drops of food coloring with 1/2 cup water and 1/2 cup vinegar in a bowl.

STEP 3: Drop the hollowed egg into the bowl. Leave it in there for as long as you'd like. (The longer it's in there, the darker the color will be.)

STEP 4: Remove the egg with the spoon and let it dry.

STEP 5: Gently fill the egg with the confetti and/or glitter (or pixie dust, if you have it).

STEP 6: Paste a piece of tissue paper over the hole to cover it.

STEP 7: Repeat with as many eggs as you'd like, perhaps making some specifically to reflect the insides of the members of your clan. Then break the eggs together to share the magic surprise inside.

QUEST

THE SCALES OF JUSTICE TREATY

POWER UNLOCKED: Fairness

BRAVERY RATING: 🔥🔥🔥🔥

Battles don't have to end with swords drawn or curses uttered. The key to resolving a squabble is to help everyone calmly recognize their differences of opinion, and also their common ground, so that they might forge the best solution.

What you'll need:
◆ **A piece of paper**
◆ **A pencil, pen, or crayon**

STEP 1: Think of a recent problem you had with someone—a friend, a sibling, a classmate, a teammate, etc. If they're around, ask them to join you. You can also make up a problem—for example, having to share a room the size of an elf's cottage with your dragon sibling.

STEP 2: Draw two overlapping circles on your paper. Label one circle with your name, the second circle with the other dragon's name, and the middle as "both."

STEP 3: Write out your side of the argument in your circle.

STEP 4: Now have the other dragon write down their side of the argument in their circle. If it's just you, put yourself in the other dragon's slippers and write down what you think their side would be.

STEP 5: Think about the common ground that exists between the two of you. This means the space where you both want the same thing, even if you have different reasons for or ways of getting there. Discuss these things and write them down in the center where your two circles overlap.

STEP 6: Using the back of the paper, write out an offering that could work for both of you. For instance, can you share or take turns with something you both want? Can you both apologize and move on?

STEP 7: Write the date and sign the treaty with your names.

Common Ground

Me

You

FINDING YOUR ROAR

Before Beppalina journeyed to find the Great Egg, she was known as Beppalina the Brave in her homeland, the Cliffs of Caraetwa. Beppalina took it upon herself to protect others. As an air dragon, she loved flying high above the Cliffs, and this allowed her to seek out those in need of her assistance. No matter who she came across—a few ground dragons being bullied by spiders (yes, spiders; like heroes, bullies come in all shapes and sizes, too), or a group of fellow air dragons practicing their wind gusts—Beppalina swooped in to help. Soon, she was known for her roars that crashed like thunder, letting everyone within a thousand miles know that she was coming. She could bellow for justice and boom for peace. There wasn't a drop of anger underneath her thick hide—Beppalina simply knew the importance of letting each of her roars speak for itself. And whenever she heard others cry out for help, she was there to turn their upset roars into happy ones.

One day, she heard a particularly sad roar carry across the wind. This was a rumble roar. She circled the Cliffs until she found a fellow air dragon slumped on a hill. The sounds of birds tweeting nearby made the dragon's low moan even more heartbreaking. Beppalina asked the dragon how she could help him. He looked up at her and sighed. Nothing could help. He was just sad.

Beppalina frowned. But of course she could help! That is what she did. That's what her bravery was for—helping! She let loose her flying roar. She could go anywhere to get something for him! The sad dragon only shook his head. Beppalina let out her negotiation roar. She could discuss any dispute he might be having with another creature! The sad dragon shook his head again. Beppalina let out her most fearsome roar— the kind she made when making her last stand to protect another. The sad dragon shook his head once more; he did not need protecting. This just happened sometimes.

Beppalina let out a roar of frustration so massive that it startled the flock of birds. Feeling guilty, she

trotted after them and saw they had perched together again on a nearby rock. That gave her an idea.

Beppalina made her way back up the hill to the sad dragon. Then she sat beside him. She listened to his sad rumble roar all evening. She did not roar back or say or do anything to try to help. She was simply there.

After a few hours, the dragon stood up and stopped his sorrowful roar. He looked at Beppalina. "It has passed," he said. His voice sounded like the fresh clip of clouds parting after a summer storm. "Thank you."

Beppalina was stunned, but she thanked the dragon in turn. She would continue to use her flying roar and her negotiation roar and her fearsome roar and all the rest to help those in need. But she would never again underestimate the power of allowing every dragon to let out their own roars, or the patience to simply be there for them.

RAISE YOUR ROAR

A roar can tell you a lot! It is important to let your roars out. But it's also important to listen to them closely and think about what they might be revealing. Perhaps you're a bit low or confused. Or maybe you have a lot of energy just bursting to be free. Once you recognize the feeling behind your roar, you'll know what your dragon heart needs!

QUIZ: What type of roar would best express your current mood?

1 Which sounds the most fun?

A. A monster rock concert
B. A fairy festival
C. A quiet evening at home with some nettle berry tea
D. A silly elf comedy show
E. None of the above

2 How will you sleep tonight?

A. I don't need sleep.
B. Like a hatchling snug in a nest
C. My wings flapping and my fangs grinding will keep me up.
D. Like a gnome in a garden
E. I'll relax a bit before it's time to sleep.

3 Do you want a new pet?

A. No, I've got a lot on my plate already!
B. Yes! Preferably something cute and cuddly!
C. I'm afraid I wouldn't be able to take care of it or it wouldn't like me.
D. Yes, so it can take me on walks and clean up after me.
E. I don't think so.

4 **There's a sunny spot on the floor of your cave. You:**

A. Don't care.
B. Bask in it.
C. Are afraid it'll burn your hide.
D. Decide it's the perfect spotlight for you to dance under.
E. Sit in the dark corner instead.

5 **What would the name of your scented candle be?**

A. Raging flames
B. Sunny fields
C. Ocean whirlpool
D. Jumping pumpkins
E. Dark cloud

6 **If you could fly anywhere right now, where would you go?**

A. The top of a tall mountain where my roars would echo
B. Somewhere fun and exciting, like the South Pole
C. A safe and familiar place, like home
D. A field of marshmallows
E. I don't think I'd go anywhere.

7 **What is your favorite type of book to read?**

A. An action story
B. A comedy
C. A mystery
D. A book of outrageous poems
E. A drama

8 **If you could choose, what color would your hide be?**

A. Red
B. Yellow
C. Invisible
D. All the colors!
E. Blue

9 **If you were—or are—a fire dragon, what would your flames be like?**

A. Bright
B. Crackling, like a small campfire
C. Smoky
D. Dancing
E. Red, orange, and blue

10 **Where would you most like to go for a swim?**

A. The sea
B. A lake
C. A river
D. A brook
E. Your tub

QUIZ RESULTS

Mostly As:

A **FEROCIOUS** roar best suits you right now. Perhaps something frustrating or bothersome has happened to irk the smoke out of your snout. But you are ready to let out your roar and release some steam. Feel free to start with a growl and then open your mouth as wide as it can go. Bellow away.

Mostly Bs:

A **COOING** roar is the best fit for you at the moment. You've got a happy, carefree spin on things and feel peaceful. Start with the hoot of an owl and then mix in the purr of a lion for the optimal coo.

Mostly Cs:

A **WHISPER** roar fits your current worries. Start with sounds like *sh*, *eek*, and *ra* in a low murmur. And don't be alarmed if your roar suddenly transforms into something else! As your uncertainty becomes clearer, the whisper often leads to other types of roars, from ferocious to squeal.

Mostly Ds:

A **SQUEAL** roar would work well for your silly mood. Make your voice as high-pitched and zany as you can. You might add a nice tune to it, too.

Mostly Es:

A **RUMBLE** roar could help express your current woes. Don't be afraid to let your rumble out—it can help any bouts of melancholy or sorrow.

QUEST

RUMBLE REPORT

POWER UNLOCKED: Intuition
BRAVERY RATING: 🔥🔥

Sometimes roars are like the weather—they can be stormy, they can be sunny, they can even be a mixture of both! When you concentrate on your feelings, you, too, can determine the various types of roars that are brewing beneath your hide.

What you'll need:

◆ A piece of paper
◆ Crayons, markers, colored pencils, etc.

STEP 1: Look over your body from snout to tail. How does it feel? Write it down or draw a picture.

STEP 2: Put your paws on your head. How does your mind feel? Write it down or draw a picture.

STEP 3: Place your paws over your heart. How does it feel? Write it down or draw a picture.

Rumble Report

STEP 4: Based on your findings, what types of roars are coming? Is there a thunderstorm of a roar on the horizon? A refreshing, sprinkling, squeaky roar? A sunny, chirpy roar with no clouds in sight? A combination? Draw a picture. Label the roar(s) that best go along with it. Maybe you can come up with a brand-new type of roar that best captures your mood.

QUEST
ROARING VOLCANO

POWER UNLOCKED: Insight
BRAVERY RATING: 🔥🔥🔥🔥

A particularly intense roar can be just like an erupting volcano! Typically, there are a few roars mixing beneath the surface that cause a forceful roar to flare. Checking in with yourself and letting out each of your roars early can help prevent them from building toward an eruption.

ASK AN
ELDER
DRAGON

What you'll need:
- ◆ **2/3 cup water**
- ◆ **4 tablespoons baking soda**
- ◆ **1 teaspoon dish soap**
- ◆ **Food coloring**
- ◆ **Some dirt or pebbles if outside; chopped nuts or damp cornmeal if inside**
- ◆ **1 cup vinegar**
- ◆ **Plastic cup**

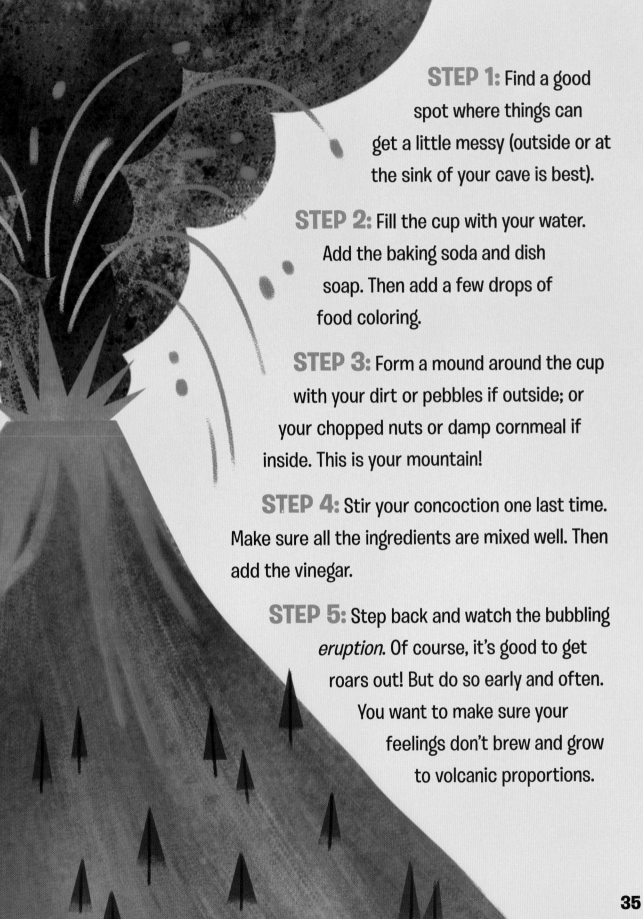

STEP 1: Find a good spot where things can get a little messy (outside or at the sink of your cave is best).

STEP 2: Fill the cup with your water. Add the baking soda and dish soap. Then add a few drops of food coloring.

STEP 3: Form a mound around the cup with your dirt or pebbles if outside; or your chopped nuts or damp cornmeal if inside. This is your mountain!

STEP 4: Stir your concoction one last time. Make sure all the ingredients are mixed well. Then add the vinegar.

STEP 5: Step back and watch the bubbling *eruption*. Of course, it's good to get roars out! But do so early and often. You want to make sure your feelings don't brew and grow to volcanic proportions.

QUEST

THE "LET GO" ROAR

POWER UNLOCKED: Strength
BRAVERY RATING: 🔥🔥🔥🔥

Getting roars out in the open before they get to unmanageable volcano status will make a world of difference in a dragon's daily quests. Whether you're nervous, angry, scared, uncertain, lost, or even bursting with happy excitement, the "Let Go" roar can help.

STEP 1: Sit in a comfy position.

STEP 2: Close your eyes and take a big deep breath in.

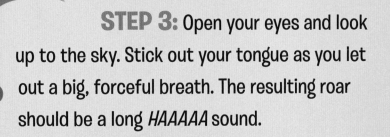

STEP 3: Open your eyes and look up to the sky. Stick out your tongue as you let out a big, forceful breath. The resulting roar should be a long *HAAAAA* sound.

STEP 4: Repeat as often as you'd like. (If you're a fire dragon: Some sparks might be released, but this should only last for a second or two.)

#3
Be brave enough to take risks that will help you grow.

SPREAD YOUR WINGS

Long ago, before Legalip reached the Great Egg, he was known as Legalip the Logical, one of the most sensible ground dragons who ever lived. He was an expert in the art of camouflage. He also happened to be a scholar and an excellent problem solver. He tutored others in geometry, calculus, and physics. Even the wisest elder dragons would seek his advice on practical matters, such as how to angle buckets to collect the most rainwater, or where to hide from fearsome predators.

But Legalip also had a secret. Though he knew many things, could solve almost any problem, and found infinite new sources of wisdom, what Legalip wanted more than anything was to fly. Now, ground dragons are perfectly capable of flying. They have wings and a good sense of direction—Legalip knew that with his knowledge of geometry and physics, he would make an excellent navigator or cartographer! The problem was, Legalip was afraid.

He tried to logic away this secret wish. He told himself he was not meant to soar through the air. He told himself that by keeping his claws rooted to the ground, he was simply protecting himself from a terrible fall. He told himself that there were thousands of things he could do on the ground—so many, in fact, that he simply didn't have time to explore the skies, too. And yet, every time he looked up at the vast blue above him, at the wispy mist that called him to come play hide-and-seek, at the flight school located just above his cavern where air dragons raced and barrel-rolled and created fluffy cloud statues of their dragon friends, he knew: He wanted to fly, but he was afraid to try.

One day, Legalip made his way to the giant tree beneath the entrance to the flight school. He could hear the other students whooping and whooshing above. "I can do this," Legalip whispered to himself. "I can *learn* to fly just like I've learned everything else." He extended his sharp claws and dug them into the tree. His limbs quaked. He could not move an inch. *No, I cannot. It's too scary, I'm afraid, it won't work*, Legalip thought. *But you want to fly*, Legalip's heart whispered. Legalip began to cry.

"What's wrong?"

Legalip turned to see an air dragon hovering next to him. "I wanted to join the flight school," he said. "I want to learn to fly but . . ."

The air dragon landed on the ground beside him. She nodded her head toward his claws gripping onto the bark. "What's stopping you?" she asked.

Me, he thought. *You*, his heart said.

Legalip looked at his strong paws gripping the tree. His claws would hold his weight and his tail would give him balance. He could climb up the tree to get to the school.

Legalip let out a determined roar. Then, very slowly, and with the air dragon hovering beside him all the way, Legalip made his way up the tree.

"Hello, everyone," the air dragon greeted the other dragons. She was, in fact, the instructor of the flight class. "We have a new student. He is a little nervous so let's give him a warm welcome." Each of the dragons flapped their wings and began to hover above the ledge.

As he watched, Legalip's wings started to twitch and he felt the cool air of the fog. His heart soared at the thought of giving it a go. His wings began to flutter. Then they began to flap. His paws rose off the ground. *I'm flying!* he thought. *You are stronger than what you fear*, Legalip's heart added.

From that day on, Legalip practiced flying every day. There were still mornings when Legalip's fear would rear its ugly head. But he would push through his discomfort with the tools in his brain and the courage in his heart, spread his wings, and glide on.

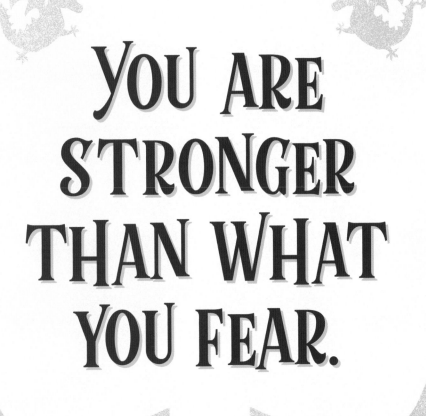

YOU ARE STRONGER THAN WHAT YOU FEAR.

TAKE A CHANCE

While spreading your wings and trying something new can make your scales shake, it can also send you soaring to the highest heights!

QUIZ: Where will spreading your wings lead you?

1 **What is one thing you want to try?**

A. Teaching little hatchlings something new

B. Making lunch for your clan

C. Performing in a play

D. Attending Camp Dragonhide for a summer

2 **Who is someone you'd like to get to know better?**

A. Dragons who live on the other side of the world

B. Yourself

C. Your teacher

D. A classmate or neighbor

3 **What would you use as the title of a book you'd write?**

A. *Lending a Helping Paw*

B. *Quests and Journeys to Spread One's Wings*

C. *Roaring for a Crowd*

D. *Sticks, Stones, and Spears: Letting Problems Roll Off Your Hide*

4 **What type of drink is the most refreshing?**

A. A jug of water

B. A cup of tea

C. A mug of Elfian hot chocolate

D. Homemade fizzy berry juice

5 **If you were to spot a flock of lost baby phoenixes, what would you do?**

A. Run around like a dragon with no snout, wanting to help but not exactly sure how

B. Rally all of your friends to help the chicks find their parents

C. Quietly ask a neighbor to lead the search

D. Make flyers for ground-dwellers to search while air dragons survey from the sky

6 **What sport sounds neat?**

A. Team paw-ball

B. Fishing à la water dragons

C. Roar-leading

D. Talons ropes course

7 **What time of day do you enjoy the most?**

A. Evening

B. High noon

C. Early morning

D. Night

8 **What can you often be found nibbling at?**

A. Spaghetti dinner

B. Snacks like chips and dip, or veggies and hummus

C. A bowl of soup

D. Marshmallows

9 **Which attribute describes you the best?**

A. Caring

B. Friendly

C. Shy

D. Hesitant

10 **If you found another dragon's treasure on the ground, you would:**

A. Ask everyone nearby if it was theirs

B. Get a search party together to hunt down the owner

C. Leave it on the ground for the dragon to find it again

D. Return home immediately to ask an elder dragon for help

QUIZ RESULTS

Mostly As:

You should try **VOLUNTEERING**! Visiting with ancient dragons in a retirement cave, fundraising for a good cause, or helping out at a soup kitchen could be just what you need to break out of your shell. It might seem a little intimidating in the moment, but try bringing a friend or an elder dragon the first few times. Odds are, your heart will be dancing afterward.

BAKE SALE

Dragon Academy Fundraiser

Mostly Bs:

Party time | me time

You should try **BEING ALONE**. You're the kind of dragon who likes to hang in a pack, but a quiet evening on your own might be a refreshing change of pace. What better way to connect with yourself and practice your unique talents?

Mostly Cs:

You should try **PUBLIC ROARING**. Perhaps giving presentations or being onstage gives your scales the heebie-jeebies. But making your roar heard can be a wonderful feeling. Who knows? You might find a fiery and zippy new passion!

Mostly Ds:

You should try out some **SURVIVAL SKILLS** and spend time in the great outdoors! Join your local dragon scouts or ask an elder for tips. Learning how to do tricky things—like tending to a fire without relying on your snout or chopping some root vegetables without your talons—can seem tough, but it can also lead to a great sense of accomplishment.

QUEST

THE ALTER EGO

POWER UNLOCKED: Creativity
BRAVERY RATING: 🔥

Sometimes it's hard to try new things or take risks. But whenever you feel nervous, you can always use your imagination to get you through. Create a dragon alter ego that you can channel in these moments. This other version of yourself might give you the roaring boost you need!

What you'll need:

◆ A mirror
◆ Blankets, scarves, hats, or any other costume pieces or props you might have (optional)

Magical Wonderful You

STEP 1: Find your birth month in the chart below and note the corresponding dragon name.

January / **Jillify**	May / **Mindeli**	September / **Seemep**
February / **Frab**	June / **Joop**	October / **Ollittan**
March / **Moorpark**	July / **Puders**	November / **Newbrangimham**
April / **Amentar**	August / **Allathew**	December / **Drakela**

STEP 2: Find the last digit of your birth date (example: a November 13 birthday would be 3). Note the corresponding attribute.

0 / **the Bold**	4 / **the Strong**	8 / **the Noble**
1 / **the Wonderful**	5 / **the Marvelous**	9 / **the Generous**
2 / **the Jolly**	6 / **the Gallant**	
3 / **the Spunky**	7 / **the Magnanimous**	

STEP 3: String the two together. Your alter ego is _____ the _____! Stand in front of the mirror and say it with gusto!

STEP 4: Create a roar for your dragon alter ego and perhaps a backstory. Are they a water dragon? A moon dragon? A ground or an air dragon? What types of sparks inspire them to let out zippy roars? Add a blanket or scarf as a new hide or cape, as well as any other costumes or props.

QUEST
LOOK INSIDE

POWER UNLOCKED: Ingenuity
BRAVERY RATING: 🔥🔥🔥🔥

Sometimes the best way to make something seem less scary is to take it apart and see what makes it work. Use those claws (and maybe a tool or two) to get started!

ASK AN ELDER Dragon

What you'll need:
- ◆ **Something you're allowed to take apart (see step 1)**
- ◆ **Tools like a screwdriver, a wrench, and/or pliers**

STEP 1: Ask an elder dragon for an old object you'd be allowed to fiddle with. Perhaps it's something lying around the cave that your clan doesn't use anymore, or a used item you can pick up at a cavern or grotto sale for cheap. Some examples could include: a plastic clock, an old toaster or radio, even a broken computer or printer. Just be sure that the elder dragon removes particularly dangerous and sparky things, like batteries and power cords.

STEP 2: Use your claws and tools (with elder dragon permission and help) to remove the exterior.

STEP 3: Once you're inside, survey the bits and pieces you find. What's connected to what? Can you guess why? What would happen if you reorganized things?

STEP 4: Tinker and play with your elder dragon's help. Now that you've seen the inner workings, it might not seem so scary to take things apart and discover what makes them tick under their hides.

FUTURE
INVENTOR

QUEST

RISK AND RE-ROARED

POWER UNLOCKED: Bravery
BRAVERY RATING: 🔥🔥🔥🔥🔥

Have you ever wondered what would happen if you tried something new or risky? What would be the best outcome? What would be the worst? It's great to prepare, but it can be equally helpful to check in *after* attempting a new power, activity, or skill as well. That way, you'll note what actually happened, as well as the benefits and drawbacks, so you know whether or not you'd do it again.

What you'll need:
◆ **A pen or pencil**
◆ **Paper**

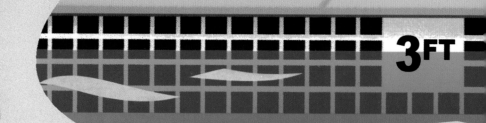

3FT

STEP 1: Take a moment to think about something that seems a little risky or nerve-wracking to you right now. Is it raising your paw in class to answer a question? Is it making a new BDF (best dragon friend)? How about starting a new project—a science experiment or perhaps a painting? Or raising money for a good cause? Maybe doing a somersault even though your tail might get in the way?

STEP 2: Use your pen and paper to write the scary thing down. Now add a goal of when you want to accomplish it. Try to pick a date that gives you enough time to practice, but isn't so far off that you'll forget.

STEP 3: Do the risky thing! Spread your wings!

STEP 4: On that same piece of paper, describe what you did and mark the date. Jot down a few sentences about how it made you feel. What, if anything, was the reward to taking that risk? What was the drawback? Repeat as many times as you'd like!

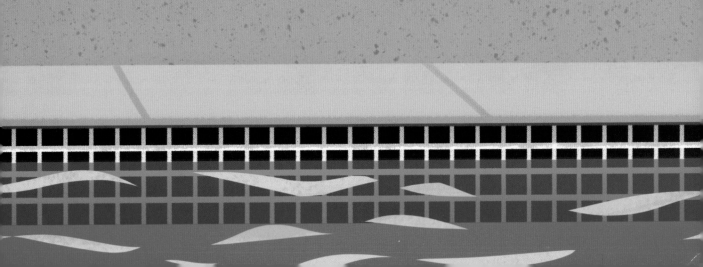

#4
Believe in yourself.

YOU ARE MAGIC

The moon dragon Kai was known as Kai the Kind, for he was kind to everyone he came across—fellow dragons, werehyenas, humans, etc. No matter where he was or what he was doing, Kai would say hello to anyone who passed, would ask how their evening was going, and would show genuine interest in the answer. Folks all across the savannah loved being around Kai because his kindness made their scales shimmer and their hearts glow. However, Kai himself had never felt the glow of his own magic. You see, most moon dragons glow when they are fully charged with joy. Kai felt perfectly happy. He loved visiting creatures all across the savannah, and his kindness and helpful nature made his heart zip with joy. But each night as he looked at his reflection under the sharp glow of the moon, he wondered if he would ever know his own glow.

One evening, Kai went for his usual walk across the savannah. He stopped to check in on some night sprites who were building new nests. He lent a paw, holding twigs here and helping place blades of grass there while the sprites sprinkled their magic dust. Kai was in awe of the nests' splendor. "You're so creative!" he exclaimed. "You've built homes that are sturdy and safe and sparkle with your magic. I wish I could do that."

Next, Kai visited an elder moon dragon who lived alone. Kai listened to story after story about the fortune-telling she had done over the years. Her hide glowed all the brighter as she remembered each dragon who came to her for help and left with hope in their hearts. "You're so helpful!" he exclaimed. "You gave each of those dragons some inspiration for the future and the magic to believe in themselves. I wish I could do that."

Finally, Kai went to watch some hatchlings at their dragon-ball match. They passed the ball on their snouts and scored three goals in a row! No one cheered harder than Kai. "You're so determined!" he exclaimed. "You've practiced and practiced and your magic simply shines under pressure. I wish I could do that."

Kai returned to his home. It had been a good day with the sprites and the elder dragon and the hatchlings. But as he sat beside the pond and stared at his reflection in the water, he thought about everyone else doing great things—building new places, telling fortunes, coming together as a team. "I don't do any of that," he said. "I have no skills or powers to speak of. Maybe that's why I don't even glow. I'm useless."

"Oh, Kai, how could you be so mean?" Kai startled. When he turned around, he saw the elder dragon being helped along by the night sprites and the hatchlings.

"What . . . what do you mean?" he asked, both in awe and in fear. He'd never been called mean in his life.

The elder dragon sat beside him and took his paws in hers. "You could never be useless," she said. "If only you would show yourself a bit of the kindness you showed me today."

"And us!" the hatchlings piped up.

"Us, too!" the sprites chimed in.

"You see, Kai? Your kindness helped to make each of our days brighter," the elder dragon said. "That's a very special kind of magic."

Kai was stunned. A smile began to make itself known to his snout. His eyes twinkled, and was that a slight shimmer on his hide? "Is that what has been missing all along?" he asked. "Showing kindness to . . . myself?"

As if in answer, Kai's coat suddenly turned a magnificent rainbow of colors. He almost had to shield his eyes by how bright it was. "Wow," he breathed. It was the most unique and colorful glow he had ever seen. "I'm . . . I'm magic!"

From then on, as he made his visits around the savannah, recognizing the magic within others, he also made sure to recognize the magic within himself.

SOMETIMES YOU HAVE TO BELIEVE IN MORE THAN MAGIC— YOU HAVE TO BELIEVE IN YOURSELF.

KNOW YOUR MAGIC

Sometimes all it takes is to acknowledge the magic you hold inside for it to really shine.

QUIZ: What color does your magic glow?

1 When faced with a challenge, you:

A. Rise up and immediately face it
B. Take a moment to come up with a good solution
C. Try to see all sides of the issue before deciding what to do
D. Ask another dragon for advice

2 What animal do you most relate to?

A. Lion
B. Parrot
C. Whale
D. Dog

3 What form of exercise sounds the most appealing?

A. Running through the forest
B. Swimming in a lake
C. Yoga to stretch your wings
D. A team sport like paw-ball

4 What trait are you most proud of?

A. Strength
B. Intelligence
C. Kindness
D. Loyalty

5 What is something you've always wanted to do?

A. Stand up for someone in the heat of the moment

B. Heal a wound instantly

C. Create something completely new

D. Make everyone around you feel great

6 The perfect vacation spot would be:

A. A bustling village where you could zip around

B. A meadow

C. Somewhere seaside

D. Wherever your clan is

7 Something you could work on is:

A. How you anger easily

B. How you get jealous

C. How you can be a little moody

D. How you are easily swayed by others

8 Your favorite birthday was:

A. When you turned 1, because everything was so new

B. When you turned 198, because you were so wise but still young

C. Ten, because it's your lucky number

D. They're all great

9 Your favorite song is:

A. A lively rock song

B. A country song

C. A folk song

D. A pop song

10 When was the last time your snout smiled?

A. When I did something I loved

B. When I put my mind to fixing something that was broken

C. When I was artistic

D. When I was surrounded by my favorite dragons

QUIZ RESULTS

Mostly As:

Your magical glow is **RED**. You have high energy and massive amounts of strength. You should focus on your zippy passions (of which you have many!) so your ego and anger don't get the best of you.

Mostly Bs:

Your magical glow is **GREEN**. You are one smart dragon and are often good at logic, science, and healing. While you can sometimes be a trickster or get green with envy, your compassionate side will often win out.

Mostly Cs:

Your magical glow is **BLUE**. You have a calming, spiritual presence and are a sensitive soul. If pushed to the brink, you can let your bad mood take over, but a nature walk or creative activity will recharge you.

Mostly Ds:

Your magical glow is YELLOW. You are often optimistic and happy, seeing the moon as half full. You thrive in the company of others and are known for being very friendly. Just make sure you trust your gut and form your own opinions as you can be easily influenced by other dragons.

QUEST

GLOW ON

POWER UNLOCKED: Resourcefulness
BRAVERY RATING: 🔥🔥

When you mix the right ingredients, you can make your magic glow even brighter!

ASK AN
ELDER
DRAGON

What you'll need:

◆ **2 bottles of glow-in-the-dark glue**
(or regular glue plus nontoxic glow-in-the-dark paint)
◆ **4 tablespoons water**
◆ **1/2 tablespoon baking soda**
◆ **Up to 2 tablespoons contact lens solution**

STEP 1: Empty your glue—and paint, if using—into a bowl.

STEP 2: Mix in the water and baking soda. You can add more water if you want the magic slime to *streeeeeeetch* like a sea serpent's neck.

STEP 3: Slowly add your contact lens solution, 1/2 tablespoon at a time. Keep an eye on the consistency to make sure it doesn't get too tough. (You might not need all of the solution.)

STEP 4: Take the slime out and knead with your paws until it's not sticky anymore.

STEP 5: Let your slime bask in some daylight for a few hours. Sometimes, it needs to charge up a bit in the warm light of kindness and confidence before it'll glow.

STEP 6: Take it into a dark cave or wait until the moon rises to see your slime glow!

QUEST

From Puzzled to Pizzazz

POWER UNLOCKED: Confidence
BRAVERY RATING: 🔥🔥🔥🔥

Sometimes when we focus on only one piece of ourselves, we miss the magic that is found in the whole dragon. Making a power puzzle can be a good reminder that we're made up of lots of different mighty parts in our scales and tails. And it can be a fun challenge to put it all back together so that you may take another look at the big picture!

ASK AN **ELDER** Dragon

What you'll need:
◆ **A thick piece of paper or an old card**
◆ **Crayons or colored pencils**
◆ **1 dark-colored marker**
◆ **Scissors (ask an elder dragon for help if needed)**

STEP 1: Draw your dragon self on your paper or on the back of an old card, using your crayons or colored pencils.

STEP 2: With the dark-colored marker, add multiple lines on top of your drawing. These will be your puzzle pieces. You can make your puzzle more challenging by drawing lots of lines (therefore creating small pieces), or you can make it easier by drawing fewer lines (creating bigger pieces). The key is to make unique shapes!

STEP 3: Write down traits you like about yourself inside the puzzle pieces. Are you kind? Do you work hard? Have you done something lately you're really proud of? These are pieces of your magic that make up the whole dragon!

STEP 4: Cut along the lines using your scissors.

STEP 5: Mix up all the pieces. Then use them to assemble your puzzle. Take another look at your self-portrait puzzle filled with your magical pizzazz! Repeat anytime you need to remember all the magic you hold within.

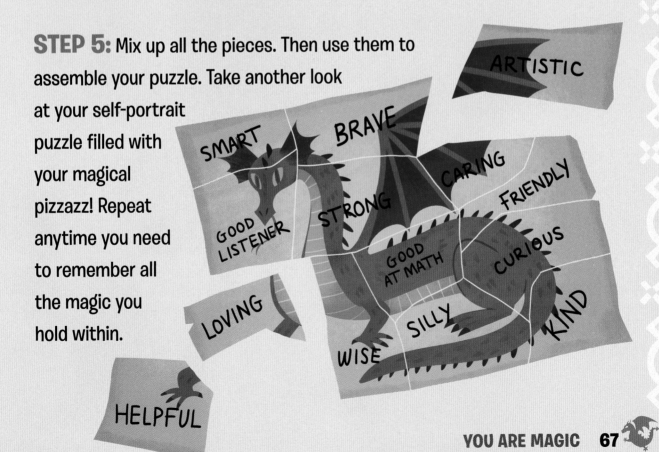

QUEST

PLANTING POSITIVITY

POWER UNLOCKED: Kindness
BRAVERY RATING: 🔥🔥🔥🔥🔥

Did you know that words have their own magic, too? When you use nice, encouraging words with someone or something, they are more likely to flourish.

What you'll need:

- ◆ Seeds (bean seeds tend to work well in many different caves and grottos)
- ◆ 2 small planting pots
- ◆ Potting soil
- ◆ Water
- ◆ Labels
- ◆ A ruler
- ◆ A piece of paper and pencil

STEP 1: Plant 2 to 3 seeds in each pot, using the potting soil and instructions on the packet.

STEP 2: Label one pot "Kindness," the other pot "Neutral."

STEP 3: Place the pots outside if it's warm, or near a sunny window if it's cold.

STEP 4: Every day, water your plants. Take the Kindness plant to another room, and say friendly, cheering things to it for 15 minutes. Afterward, put the Kindness plant back in its spot.

STEP 5: Then, take the Neutral plant to the other room for 15 minutes, but do not say anything to it. Once the time has run out, put it back in its spot.

STEP 6: Log your findings on your piece of paper every day for a week. Use the ruler to see how much each plant grows. Make a note of it. Record how each plant looks: Does it seem green and healthy? Droopy and small? Is it reaching to the sky or curling down toward the ground?

STEP 7: After a week, examine your findings. What power did the kind words seem to have? How can you apply this to yourself and the dragons in your life?

#5
Do what you love.

Find Your Spark

When Zadie the Zippy was a young fire dragon living on the island of Thoemgi, she would get up early every morning to let out some steam and do some deep fire breathing. She'd breathe deep into her belly until she was calm. Then she'd practice painting the sky with her flames. She could make a pineapple, her favorite breakfast food. She could make a ukulele, her brother Juju's favorite instrument. But she wanted to create something bigger, something better, something more.

One day, her friend Mopo found her on the beach. "Do you want to play volleyball with me?" Mopo asked. Mopo loved spiking the ball with her tail and let out happy roars as she played.

"I can play for a little while," Zadie said. "Then maybe we could play fire charades?"

"Oh," Mopo said. "I don't know. . . . Fire breathing isn't really for me. I'm trying to perfect my serve! It'll make me *sooo* zippy if I can land it with my tail."

Zadie agreed to play volleyball with her friend. But it never got her heart racing or her snout smiling like it did for Mopo.

Later that day, Zadie found Juju on the beach, strumming his ukulele with his talons. Zadie bopped her head to the music. But she didn't let out joyful roars like Juju did as he wrote a new tune.

"Do you want to play fire charades with me?" Zadie asked Juju after the fifth song.

"No, not today," Juju said. "I'm auditioning to be part of the Rock 'n' Roar band!"

Zadie said he'd be perfect for the gig. Then she made her way to a distant cove on the beach. She sat down and began to breathe.

"Everyone has something they're practicing," she said. "Everyone has something to share. Except me." Zadie sat in the sand for a long time, taking in big deep breaths, but swallowing down the flames that wanted to come out in great vibrant shapes. She still wanted to create something bigger, something better, something more. But, she wondered, what was the point?

The sun was beginning to set when Zadie heard a soft shuffling over the sand. She turned and saw her dad and Juju coming across the beach, a picnic basket being carried between them. Zadie's dad was an expert cook. He made something new and creative and tasty for dinner every night. Sometimes Zadie used her fire breath to help roast vegetables, watching him mix and stir and season with a smile.

"Juju said you seemed down," Zadie's dad said. He and Juju set the basket on the ground and he began to serve up plates of food.

"Dad, does cooking making you zippy?" she asked him. "Like playing the ukulele makes Juju zippy, or practicing a serve makes Mopo zippy?

Zadie's dad smiled. "Yes, I believe it does!"

Zadie nodded slowly. "I wish I had a spark," she said. "I must be the only dragon who doesn't have one."

"But you get up every morning before anyone else to practice your fire breathing," Zadie's dad said.

"And you're always asking to play fire charades," Juju chimed in.

"And," their dad continued, "if I'm not mistaken, you've been sitting out here all evening practicing your deep breathing, yes?"

Zadie nodded. But she didn't quite follow what they were trying to say.

"Zadie," her dad said softly, "a spark is anything that brings you joy. Just because something doesn't make everyone zippy, it doesn't mean it can't be yours."

"Do you mean . . . what do you mean?" she asked.

"Your spark is about *you*," her dad said.

Zadie didn't know many other dragons, even other fire dragons, who practiced fire breathing as much as she did. She rose with the sun to practice breathing. She knew how to breathe deeply for calm, and even deeper to light the fire deep within her belly. She practiced breathing in fast bursts and slow streams. She even practiced holding her breath so that one day she might be able to test her endurance and release a stream of fire for as long as an hour!

Zadie stood up from her seat and backed away from the beach picnic. Then she took a slow, deep breath. She let it fill her up from her head to her paws and waited to feel the fire light in her belly. Then she tipped her head toward the sky and began to let out her breath.

Zadie's dad and Juju *oohed* and *aahed* as they watched the flames take the shape of one, two, three dragons and a picnic dinner of grilled pineapple kebabs and fire-roasted fish and strawberry sundaes.

"Zadie!" her dad exclaimed. "Look what you've made! How did you learn to do that?"

"I practiced," Zadie said. She'd never felt more zippy. She didn't need to find a spark; she'd had one all along.

SPARK A PASSION

It might take trying out a few different activities to find your spark. The trick is to see what makes you feel like letting out zippy roars!

QUIZ: What passion should you fly toward?

1 **What's your favorite type of video to watch online?**

A. A crazy paw-ball dunk
B. A colorful music video
C. A funny cat video
D. A how-to-build-it video

2 **What is your favorite subject in school?**

A. PE
B. Art
C. Health
D. Robotics

3 **What do you do every night before bed?**

A. Run around the cave
B. Read a book
C. Snuggle with your enchanted wolf pup
D. Work on your latest project

4 **If you had a box of markers, which color would you grab?**

A. Red
B. Purple
C. Green
D. Orange

5 **What's your favorite after-school snack?**

A. A forest bite (recipe on page 148)
B. Cheese, crackers, and grapes
C. Ants on a log
D. A sandwich

6 **Who would you want to spend an afternoon with?**

A. A team of volleyball players
B. A band of musicians
C. Chefs
D. Fire breathers

7 **Which place makes you happiest?**

A. Anywhere you can be outside
B. A stage
C. An animal shelter
D. A lab

8 **Every morning, you:**

A. Hop on one paw to get your blood pumping
B. Write in your journal
C. Take your enchanted wolf pup for a flight
D. Use your homemade electric toothbrush to get the fangs in the back

9 **What's the best part about a birthday party?**

A. Swinging at the constellation, egg-shaped piñata
B. Singing "Happy Birthday"
C. Hanging out with friends
D. The games

10 **To get to school, you'd rather:**

A. Walk or fly
B. Take the bus so you can draw
C. Ride the back of a yeti
D. Drive the cart you fixed up

QUIZ RESULTS

Mostly As:

Your next spark is something **ATHLETIC**. From biking to rock climbing to team sports, you seem to enjoy physical activity. Start a flying, hiking, or running club, or join a paw-ball team. Your roars will start sounding zippy in about as long as it takes you to soar around the block and back.

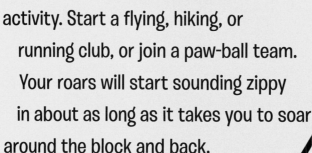

Mostly Bs:

Your next spark is something **ARTISTIC**. Whether you're a musician, a painter, an actor, or a writer, you shine when you're doing something imaginative. Enroll in an acting or writing class, or pick up a new instrument to get those creative 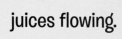 juices flowing.

Mostly Cs:

Your next spark is something to do with **NATURE**. Perhaps you're a big animal lover, or you just really like being in the great outdoors. You might find your passion starting a raijū-walking business or volunteering at the local zoo. And the animals sure will sense the zippiness you're feeling.

Mostly Ds:

Your next spark is something in **TECH**. You're an engineer at heart and love to find new ways to tinker and make things. Join a robotics club or take a computer class. Who knows—your passion might lead to the next great invention and you could end up with a Noble *Nobel Creature* Prize!

QUEST
DREAM SPARKS

POWER UNLOCKED: Zippiness
BRAVERY RATING: 🔥🔥🔥🔥

Every dragon has their own unique passions and sparks. Sometimes it helps to let your sparks and dreams collide to help you stay focused on what makes you feel zippy.

ASK AN ELDER DRAGON

What you'll need:
- ◆ Sheets of blank paper
- ◆ Scissors
- ◆ Hole puncher
- ◆ Yarn
- ◆ Tape
- ◆ Colored pencils, crayons, markers, paints, glitter, confetti, and anything else you'd like to decorate with

STEP 1: Fold and cut your sheets of paper into four pieces.

STEP 2: On each piece, write down one of your sparks. It could be something you love to do already, or something you'd like to try in the future. Anything that makes you feel zippy!

STEP 3: Decorate each piece of paper with the glitter or confetti, and make them as colorful as you'd like.

STEP 4: Use the hole puncher to make a hole at the top of each piece of paper.

STEP 5: Add a loop of yarn to the top of each piece of paper so you can hang them in the perfect spot—maybe above your bed or beside your work space.

STEP 6: Be sure to revisit your dream sparks any time you need a little inspiration to try something new, or to remember what makes you feel zippy.

QUEST
MAKE NEW SPARKS

POWER UNLOCKED: Passion
BRAVERY RATING: 🔥🔥🔥

Sparks, like dragons, can change over time. You can try a new activity anytime you need to let out some zippy roars. Remember, stepping outside your comfort zone may seem scary at first, but it can lead to the greatest discoveries.

What you'll need:
- A piece of paper
- A pen or pencil

STEP 1: Make a spark chart by dividing your piece of paper into three columns: "Date," "Activity," and "Zippy Level."

STEP 2: Try three different activities this month. They can be things you've done before, something you've tried but weren't sure about, or maybe even your BDF's (Best Dragon Friend) favorite activity.

STEP 3: After each activity, check in with yourself. Is your heart racing in a good way? Do you want to let out a joyful roar? Would you try this activity again?

STEP 4: Write down the date, the activity, and your zippy levels from 1 to 10 afterward. If you repeat activities, you may find those levels change depending on the day, your mood, and what happened. But if you find that you're feeling pretty zippy and ready to let out those happy roars most of the time, you have probably discovered a spark!

QUEST

FIND A GUIDE

POWER UNLOCKED: Determination
BRAVERY RATING: 🔥🔥🔥

Sometimes it's helpful to find other dragons who share the same passion as you and see what they have done to pursue their sparks. Learning more about their quests can help you on yours.

ASK AN
ELDER
DRAGON

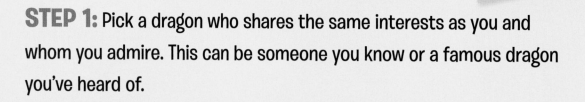

What you'll need:
◆ Access to a computer or a library

STEP 1: Pick a dragon who shares the same interests as you and whom you admire. This can be someone you know or a famous dragon you've heard of.

STEP 2: Find out as much information about this dragon as you can. If they are someone you know, see if you can do an interview with them and ask them for tips. Ask about the things they were doing when they were your age or level of activity to practice their sparks, and if there's anything else you should try or keep in mind. Maybe there's information they wish they'd had much earlier, too! (This type of elder dragon wisdom is a treasure in itself.) If they are someone you don't know, hop online (with elder dragon permission, of course) or go to the library to see what you can learn about them.

STEP 3: Note the things that seem interesting or helpful to you. Is there anything these dragon guides did or do that you can do, too? For example, can you write in a journal every day? Can you try a new sport or learn how to play chess? Can you start your own weekend science experiments or make short films in the back of your cave? Is there a certain frame of mind these dragons recommend having? Are there things to consider when you're not able to do as much as you'd like with your spark? Let this guide help in your quest for zippiness!

#6
Take good care of
yourself so you can
take care of others.

GUARD YOUR TREASURE

Many moons ago, Jabber the Just was just a water dragon from the Peadella peninsula. He liked feeling calm and relaxed. He loved floating about and finding colorful shells. He also enjoyed taking his time to examine everything—coral, kelp, sea books—from all angles. One day, he heard some arguing outside of his grotto. Swimming over to investigate, he found two water dragons arguing over a piece of star cucumber.

"I found it so I should be the one to have it," one of the water dragons explained.

"You found this treasure in front of *my* sea cove," the other water dragon chimed in. "Therefore it should be mine."

Jabber thought for a moment. "You each have a point and an equal claim to this treasure. I believe the fair thing to do would be to cut the star cucumber in half so you both can enjoy it."

The dragons blinked at him and then look at each other. "We never thought of that!" one of the dragons said. "Good idea," the other said.

So Jabber cut the star cucumber and handed the equal pieces to both dragons, who thanked him for his help.

Soon word spread about Jabber's ability to look at a problem from all sides and offer a fair solution. Creatures would travel far and wide to ask him to solve all sorts of problems. The merfolk needed a schedule for when they could blast their favorite music and not bother their neighbors. A local school of fish had to find a new location for a watercolor club. Someone had to ask a particularly enthusiastic water dragon to hold off from rain roaring at least one day a week so that a ground dragon's hydrangeas could grow.

One day, a new problem arrived that wasn't so easily solved. Jabber started to feel off, and he wasn't sure why. Sure, he was very busy and found himself getting home to his sea cove later and later. But he liked helping other creatures.

The next day, he worked from sunup to sundown, solving one problem after the next. He was so good at helping to solve problems that he didn't realize how quickly the time passed or how many creatures he'd seen until he got home. His head ached. His paws were sore from cheering each problem solved. His heart was weary.

In the morning, he ignored his alarm and the critters knocking at his door. He stayed in bed until he was ready to start the day. He made his favorite seaweed pancakes for breakfast. Then he took his favorite book—*The Adventures of Merlock Holmes*—out to his favorite rock in the cove where he could lie half in the shade, half in the sun and read all day long.

"What's Jabber doing?" some of the merfolk whispered.

"Why is he ignoring us today?" the fairies asked.

"Does he still want to be our friend?" the fish wondered out loud.

The crowd around his rock had grown so large that, finally, Jabber put his book aside and sat up. "Of course I'm still your friend," he said. "And I'm not ignoring you today. But after looking at the problem from all sides, I've realized that I cannot help you take care of your needs if I do not take care of myself."

Jabber had been so focused on helping others find creative solutions to guard their treasures, he'd lost track of his own—the treasure buried inside of him. He had forgotten how much he liked to take things slow, how important it was for his body to feel calm and relaxed, how much he loved floating. Then, Jabber slid into the water to float. And to his surprise, the merfolk and the fish floated right alongside him while the fairies hovered above. From that day on, one day a week, the creatures needing some comfort would gather at Jabber's sea cove. There, they would spend the afternoon looking up at the sky as they floated, refreshing their own particular magic and treasures in the company of their friends.

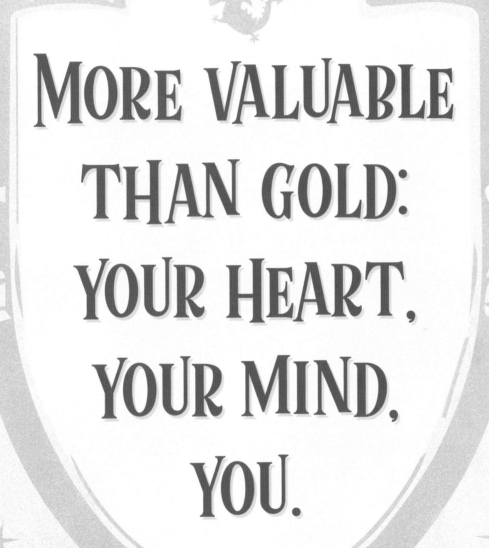

MORE VALUABLE
THAN GOLD:
YOUR HEART,
YOUR MIND,
YOU.

REFRESH, RENEW, RESTORE

It's important for every dragon to guard their most precious treasures by figuring out what makes you feel good, what helps you be the very best dragon you can be, and to carve out time for it even on the busiest day.

QUIZ: What's a good way for you to unwind?

1 **When you're at a shell-ebration or party, you:**

A. Like to chat with a small group

B. Race around the cove until you've hit every nook and cranny of the shindig

C. Chat with the elders and also play with the little hatchlings

D. Play a rousing game of charades

2 **What gives you the most energy?**

A. Taking deep, calming breaths

B. Flying, swimming, or running

C. Family barbecues and roasts

D. Watching a heist or mystery movie

3 What sounds the coziest?

A. A soft blanket
B. Fuzzy socks for your paws
C. A beach bonfire
D. A mug of nettle berry tea

4 What would you rather gaze at?

A. A sunset
B. A sunrise
C. A cloudless sky
D. A full moon

5 What do you like to do during lunchtime?

A. Eat a delicious meal
B. Gallop around the track
C. Hang out with friends
D. Head to the library

6 What is the best type of pizza?

A. Pineapple
B. Veggie
C. Half cheese, half pepperoni
D. White pizza with spinach and broccoli

7 If you weren't a dragon, what animal would you be?

A. Bear
B. Cheetah
C. Whale
D. Monkey

8 What's your favorite dragon ability?

A. Cloaking
B. Flying
C. Roaring
D. Future-telling

9 What's your ideal holiday?

A. One where you get some time off
B. One with lots of time outdoors for nature hiking
C. One where you have a big family dinner
D. One with a good story behind it

10 What's one word that describes you?

A. Smart
B. Fast
C. Loyal
D. Imaginative

QUIZ RESULTS

Mostly As:

You could use some **ALONE TIME**! While you enjoy the company of other dragons, having some quiet time to check in with yourself is what helps refuel your tank. Try meditating or taking a warm bath (bubble balls encouraged).

Mostly Bs:

You should try some rousing **EXERCISE**. Whether it be playing a sport, flying about, or going for a nice swim, when you get your blood pumping, you gain more energy. The next time you're feeling low, dust off those dragon trainers and get going.

Mostly Cs:

One way you can really kick back is by spending some time with your **CLAN**. You thrive off the energy of others, especially those you're closest to, like your family and friends. Make plans to hang out and watch your roars and mood improve!

Mostly Ds:

You'll feel more refreshed after enjoying a good **STORY**. This could be something like a good book or movie, but getting lost in another world is just what the dragon-doctor ordered. Ask a friend for a good recommendation and curl up with a nice escape for a little while.

QUEST

BUBBLE BALL

POWER UNLOCKED: Self-love
BRAVERY RATING: 🔥🔥

Caring for yourself and honoring the treasure within are as important as any of your other heroic duties. A bubble ball makes bath time all the more rejuvenating. This could be just what you need to slow down and polish the treasure beneath your hide.

ASK AN ELDER Dragon

What you'll need:

- 1 cup baking soda
- 1/2 cup Epsom salt
- 1/2 cup citric acid (you can also substitute lemon juice)
- 3/4 cup cornstarch
- 2 tablespoons coconut oil (ask the elder dragon helping you to melt it on the stove, or with some fire breath)
- 6 teaspoons water
- 2 teaspoons natural essential oils (let your elder dragon know that chamomile and lavender are favorite relaxing options)
- Natural food coloring
- Plastic eggs or greased muffin tins

STEP 1: Mix the baking soda, Epsom salt, citric acid, and cornstarch in a bowl.

STEP 2: In a separate small bowl, mix the coconut oil, water, essential oils, and food coloring.

STEP 3: Slowly incorporate your wet ingredients into your dry. (Be gentle or you might take all the fizziness out of your bubble ball when it comes time to use it.) Once it takes on the consistency of wet sand, you can knead it together with your paws.

STEP 4: Roll into balls and pack them into the plastic eggs or greased muffin tin. Let them set for at least 24 hours.

STEP 5: Use a spoon to gently tap your mold (the eggs or muffin tin), to get the bubble balls out in one piece. They should feel nice and firm.

STEP 6: Enjoy the fizzing, great-smelling, colorful water in your next bath!

QUEST

A Breath of Fresh Air

POWER UNLOCKED: Peace
BRAVERY RATING: 🔥

Sometimes we need a moment to check in with our breath—be it ocean, fire, or otherwise. Think of your breath as a nice wind gust in your belly, helping that inner treasure soar to new heights.

What you'll need:

◆ **A quiet spot**　　　　◆ **Pillows, blankets**

STEP 1: Get comfy in your quiet spot with your pillows, blankets, or anything else that makes you feel cozy.

STEP 2: Close your eyes.

STEP 3: Focus on your breath. Imagine every inhale is a gentle wave coming into your cove, and every exhale is the wave going out with the tide.

STEP 4: Keeping your breaths long and ocean-deep, start to shift your focus to your body. Start with your paws. Squeeze them with your inhale, release them on your exhale. Then slowly work your way up. Squeeze your tail, release. Squeeze your belly, release. Do this all the way up to your face and snout.

STEP 5: Return to your breath and its waves. Open your eyes. Notice how you feel. Are you ready to let out a roar? What kind?

STEP 6: Repeat whenever you feel like you need a moment to refresh, collect yourself, and check in with the roars you need to let out.

Breathe

QUEST

Do the Dragon Dance

POWER UNLOCKED: Energy
BRAVERY RATING: 🔥🔥🔥

Some dragons need to get their blood pumping and their wings flapping to feel their best. And there's no better way to feel that energy coursing from snout to tail than by doing the dragon dance.

What you'll need:
- ◆ **Music**
- ◆ **Space to move**

STEP 1: Turn on an upbeat song.

STEP 2: Hold your paws in front of you. Jump to the left. Jump to the right. Bounce around in a circle.

STEP 3: Repeat.

STEP 4: Leap to the left with your claws pointed to the sun.

STEP 5: Leap to the right with your claws pointed to the ground.

STEP 6: Twist all the way down.

STEP 7: Leap; leap; show your teeth!

STEP 8: Repeat steps 1 to 7 as many times as you'd like. Feel free to add your own moves, and invite other dragons to join you, too!

#7
Be the one and only YOU.

Show Yourself

Millow the Marvelous lived in the bustling snowy mountain village of Broom with her fellow air dragons and other winter-loving creatures. She had many interests— baking cookies with elves, skating on the frozen pond with a couple of reindeer, making snow-dragons with some hatchlings. But her favorite thing to do when she was alone in her house with the windows closed and the curtains drawn was to sing. Millow would find herself roaring out a tune as she made her breakfast or humming a sweet lullaby before bed. And every Tuesday, she'd cloak herself to make sure she was not seen, then she'd fly down to the village square to watch the Snow Bells choir rehearse. They sounded so pretty, and they looked like they were having fun. But the very thought of singing in front of anyone else made Millow's fur stand on end and her snout let out nervous roars.

One afternoon, as Millow watched the choir practice a new song, she was so lost in the music that she began belting out the chorus. Some other dragons turned to stare. The choir stopped singing mid high note. Millow finished the chorus and was about to start the next verse when she heard it. Silence. She looked at the choir and other spectators who were all staring at her. She looked down. Her snowy white tail and her claws and her proud chest and her snout were all visible.

Millow had never been so embarrassed. Immediately, she tried to cloak again. But she couldn't do it. She stood there in the village square, the last of her high notes still echoing off the mountains around them, completely and totally exposed.

Millow flew home and triple-locked the door behind her. She couldn't believe she'd been seen. And heard *singing*!

From that moment on, Millow found herself using her cloaking ability more and more. Before it had just been something she did while watching the choir, but cloaking became her normal state of being. No matter where she was—flying through the air, roaming through the snow-flocked ground, or even standing smack dab in the middle of a winter festival—Millow blended in with her surroundings and moved about undetected.

Then, one Tuesday morning as Millow was washing the dishes, humming a happy tune, she heard a chorus. And it wasn't just any chorus. The entire Snow Bells choir was standing on her doorstep singing the same song they'd been singing when Millow had joined in.

Millow wasn't sure what to do. She was nervous and afraid and overjoyed and happy all at once. She tried to cloak but only her bottom half would hide. The rest of her stood tall and proud. Slowly, Millow opened the door.

The Snow Bells finished their song and started another. They sang and sang until finally Millow joined in. First, she just moved her snout to the words. Then she sang on key but so softly that even the mice couldn't hear her. It took two hours and eight songs before Millow was belting out the notes in perfect harmony with all the rest.

"You have a beautiful voice," one of the elves piped up.

"That's very true," the choir director said. "Why did you hide when you came to watch us practice? You could have joined in."

Millow felt even more embarrassed now. She knew her tail was tucked firmly between her legs, even though it was still cloaked and none of the others could see it.

"I've always felt too shy to join," she said. "I love to sing, but I didn't know if I'd fit in."

One of the reindeer nodded. "I felt shy before I became one of the tenors. But everyone in the group is really encouraging. We have a lot of fun. And you were marvelous! What a crescendo!"

"Would you like to join the Snow Bells choir? We could use a big voice like yours," the director said.

Millow realized she'd already done the hard thing once—she'd sung for the choir in the village square. They'd seen her from top to tail, singing with all the air she could breathe and . . . she was happy. Nothing made her happier than singing. "I would love to join!" she said. She was so happy, in fact, that her bottom half revealed itself and her tail brightened, pointing straight up to the sky.

And so, Millow did something she hadn't done in a while: She stopped cloaking. Everyone in all of Broom saw her giant, glinting smile as she soared through the skies. They heard her booming voice lilt over the wind. They watched her perform with the Snow Bells choir at the annual concert and everyone agreed—the choir had never sounded better.

Stand tall.
Speak up.
Show the
World What
You're Made of.

SHOW AND SHINE

Sometimes the bravest thing a dragon can do is show yourself exactly as you are. Let yourself shine from top to tail!

QUIZ: What dragon power should you showcase more often?

1 What's your favorite season?

A. Winter
B. Spring
C. Summer
D. Fall

2 Where can other dragons find you at a picnic?

A. Leading a sing-along
B. Playing a game of paw-ball
C. Examining the wildlife
D. Chatting with others

3 You pride yourself on your:

A. Perfect pitch (musically speaking)
B. Super speed
C. Intelligence
D. Creativity

4 At a grotto sale, you'd most like to buy:

A. A flute or clarinet
B. Weights
C. A robot
D. A paint palette

5 **Your favorite mythical animals are:**

A. Phoenixes
B. Sphinxes
C. Big foots (ahem, *feet*)
D. Hippogriffs

6 **Your favorite type of weather is:**

A. Crisp, windy days
B. Sunshine
C. Tropical rain
D. Snow

7 **You love eating:**

A. Hot soup
B. Noodles
C. A fancy three-course meal
D. Pudding

8 **What type of puzzles do you like best at clan game night?**

A. Trivia
B. Colored cubes
C. Jigsaw
D. Crossword

9 **The activity you'd rather <u>not</u> do is:**

A. Hiking
B. Listen to classical music
C. Paint
D. Code

10 **What is your favorite accessory?**

A. Necklace
B. Hat
C. Sunglasses
D. Bracelet

QUIZ RESULTS

Mostly As:

You should let your **WIND GUSTS** out more! Whether in the form of singing, playing musical instruments, or performing long monologues, your dragon lungs are quite impressive. Don't be afraid to fill them up and let out those gusty roars!

Mostly Bs:

You should showcase your **SUPER STRENGTH**! You have a knack for sports and martial arts, and can lift the heaviest of objects, like trees and boulders. Flex those muscles or join a team to let your power shine!

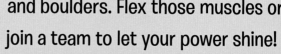

Mostly Cs:

You should reveal your uncanny ability with **CHARMS**. From building to designing to coding, you have a lot of magic going on in that head of yours. Who knows—if you perform an experiment out in the open, it might end up doing something totally innovative for your whole clan!

Mostly Ds:

You should share your **FUTURE-TELLING**! From writing stories to painting pictures to composing lyrics and poetry, your ability to spin a yarn—especially one that will one day come true in some shape or form—is impressive. Don't be afraid to showcase your work!

QUEST

DAZZLE AND GLOW

POWER UNLOCKED: Confidence
BRAVERY RATING: 🔥🔥

Sometimes in order to show yourself, you need to know your own glow. Wash off your hide to reveal the shining you and all your sparks underneath.

ASK AN ELDER Dragon

What you'll need:
- ◆ 1 cup oatmeal
- ◆ 6 tablespoons plain yogurt
- ◆ 6 tablespoons honey
- ◆ A towel

STEP 1: Make the oatmeal according to the instructions on the package. Let it cool.

STEP 2: Mix the yogurt and honey in a bowl. Fold the oatmeal into it.

STEP 3: Apply the mixture to your face and snout, making sure to avoid your eyes. Leave it on for 10 to 15 minutes.

STEP 4: Wash the scrub off with a towel to find those fresh glowing scales underneath!

Shine BRIGHT

QUEST

Self-Portrait

POWER UNLOCKED: Reflection
BRAVERY RATING: 🔥

Sometimes sharing your magic with others comes naturally. Other times, it can feel like the scariest quest of all. But it's good to remind yourself of the many gifts you have to share with the world.

What you'll need:
◆ **A piece of paper**
◆ **Markers, crayons, or colored pencils**
◆ **Glitter or confetti**
◆ **Glue**
◆ **Tape**

STEP 1: Using a marker, crayon, or colored pencil, draw a picture of your dragon self. Feel free to use different colors to get your hide—as well as your glow—exactly right. Be sure to add your wings,

too, and you can color them in or decorate them with your glitter or confetti. Show yourself doing something that makes you feel zippy.

STEP 2: Once you have your portrait done, add items around the picture that reflect your talents, hobbies, dreams, and goals. Be sure to add some colorful details, and maybe some glitter or confetti, too.

STEP 3: Find a place to hang your portrait where you can see it every day. Maybe it's beside your bed, or next to your work space, or on the refrigerator if you want to share it with your clan.

STEP 4: You can repeat Steps 1, 2, and 3 as you grow and change and find new sparks or passions to make you feel zippy.

WHERE THE WIND TAKES YOU

Sometimes you need an extra push to fly outside your comfort zone. When you're not feeling very brave, why not let the wind nudge you in the right direction? It can make the journey more fun!

What you'll need:
◆ **Space to move around**

STEP 1: Find your birth month in the chart and note the corresponding windy adjective.

January / **Strong**	April / **Fresh**	July / **Wild**	October / **High**
February / **Gentle**	May / **Blustery**	August / **Brisk**	November / **Fast**
March / **Heavy**	June / **Rainy**	September / **Warm**	December / **Light**

STEP 2: Find the last digit of your birth date (example: a November 13 birthday would be 3). Note the corresponding type of wind.

0 / **Breeze**	2 / **Draft**	4 / **Hurricane**	6 / **Flurry**	8 / **Headwind**
1 / **Gust**	3 / **Gale**	5 / **Puff**	7 / **Current**	9 / **Tailwind**

STEP 3: String the two words together. The wind you'll be using for your travel today is: a _____ _____.

STEP 4: Think of a situation where it might seem a little nerve-wracking to show yourself. Examples could be a birthday party with other dragons you don't know very well yet, or a presentation at school.

STEP 5: Spin in a circle five times fast. Then spin in the other direction five times fast.

STEP 6: Let your specific type of wind move you to that imaginary situation. Pretend you've just arrived and let out your bravest roar!

STEP 7: Repeat whenever you need the extra boost to get out of your comfort zone.

Start Where You Are

Dexter the Dedicated was a fire dragon who lived in the desert village of Wakeal with a great big clan. He spent his days hiking and taking lessons in age-shifting (transforming from a hatchling to a 1,728-year-old dragon was quite fun). On weekends, he would use his fire breath to bake his favorite dragon cake.

One day, his closest cousins, Weelem and Wana, came to tell him that the clan was holding a reunion in a few days' time. Hundreds of distant relatives would flock to Wakeal to meet, mingle, and compete in a bunch of fire-breathing games. This was the first time the whole clan had all been together in centuries. Weelem and Wana asked if he wanted to practice fire breathing with them so they'd be ready for all the games, but Dexter declined. He had some sand-dune hiking to do, as well as some cake-eating. Besides, he didn't really need practice. He thought his fire breathing was pretty great. He could even let out rare blue sparks.

When the day of the big reunion arrived, Dexter climbed the sand dunes excitedly. He couldn't wait to participate in the games and show off his blue flame. He watched a trio test a ring toss, breathing gigantic flames perfectly through each hoop. Dexter's jaw dropped. He'd never let out a flame that big. He turned his attention to some others creating an obstacle course before blowing long, focused fire trails that zigged and zagged around the cones. Dexter's heart sank. He had never let out a trail like that before. Then he turned his head and saw the worst thing yet—a few dragons letting out blue sparks. And then green ones and purple and pink! He gasped.

Dexter hurried back to his cave. He'd never felt more . . . behind. Roaring flames, making trails, changing the color of his sparks had come easily to him. But now that he knew there was more. . . . He took a deep breath and—nothing came out. Panicked, Dexter tried again. This time, he forgot the most basic rule of fire breathing and didn't open his mouth. He sputtered out some smoke. Dexter cried out in frustration. He'd always been a natural at fire breathing. But seeing what the rest of his clan could do only made him feel like he should find a brand-new spark. Maybe something his family hadn't tried before, like a dandelion-eating contest or reading a lot of books.

Feeling like he could not show his fireless snout to the clan, Dexter hid in his cave all morning and into the afternoon. When Weelem and Wana

came looking for him, he had worked himself into such a state that they could hardly coax him out of his cave.

"What are you doing?" Weelem asked. "You're missing all the fun."

"Yeah, you should see Great-Aunt Nessie do the fire Hula-Hoop!" Wana added.

But that only made Dexter cry out even louder. "I can't do it!" he wailed. "I will never be a good enough fire breather."

"What do you mean?" his cousins asked at the same time.

"You're an excellent fire breather," Weelem said.

"And you make the best cake in all the clan with your fire breath," Wana added.

Dexter dried his eyes. "You mean, there's more to fire breathing than the tricks? I can't do the Hula-Hoop. Or shoot flames up to the sky. Or—"

"Of course there's more than tricks! There are a few 230-year-olds out there who are breathing smoke," Weelem said. "But we're all just out there having fun, not comparing our skills to the others'."

"And if you really want to get better at something, what better way than to ask that dragon to teach you?" Wana added.

Dexter grinned from ear to ear. "I would love that!"

So Dexter and his cousins joined the rest of the clan for the reunion, and Dexter immediately wished he'd gone out sooner. He had the time of his life meeting the other dragons, listening to some of the best stories he'd ever heard, and eating his favorite family recipes. Great-Aunt Nessie even wanted to know how he'd made the best dragon cake she'd ever tasted. (One great blast of heat so the inside stays soft and gooey.) And when he was asked to join the fire-breathing games, he decided to face the challenge instead of fly away from it. After a few rounds and some tips from the other dragons, Dexter actually managed to roar out the biggest blue flicker he ever had, prompting cheers from the crowd.

From then on, Dexter learned to share his many sparks instead of comparing his to others. And with a little help from his large clan, he even learned to do the Hula-Hoop just as well as Great-Aunt Nessie.

PRACTICE PERSISTENCE

When a spark doesn't come naturally, or you're comparing yourself to others, a task can feel more challenging. It's frustrating when you don't get something on the first try, but practicing as much as you can and getting support from some loved ones will help. If you love something, keep at it!

QUIZ: What type of dragon problem-solving do you most respond to?

1 What's your favorite way to eat dragon cake?

A. Slowly so you can savor every bite
B. Cutting it up so that every piece has a bit of frosting and filling
C. With your clan
D. At the end of the party, after all the other activities

2 Do you make your bed or nest?

A. When I have time
B. Yes, and I clean the rest of my room as well.
C. When someone asks me to
D. Not usually; there are too many other things to do.

3 **What types of tunes get your tail grooving?**

A. Slow ballads
B. Rap songs
C. Folk songs
D. Oldies

4 **Who would you say is your BDF (Best Dragon Friend)?**

A. A sibling
B. A childhood friend
C. An elder dragon or a parent
D. Yourself

5 **Whenever you get a new appliance for your cave that requires some tricky assembly, you:**

A. Give up within the first five minutes of trying to put it together
B. Hammer a couple of pieces together and cross your claws
C. Work on it all day and all night by yourself
D. Go through every step in the instruction manual twice

6 **During a storm, you like to:**

A. Curl up by a cozy fire you've breathed and relax
B. Solve a lengthy puzzle
C. Play games with your clan
D. Go for a walk in the rain

7 **What would be your best animal sidekick?**

A. Sloth
B. Rabbit
C. Dolphin
D. Dog

8 **What would you like to be when you are an elder dragon?**

A. A musician
B. A surgeon
C. A social worker
D. A writer

9 **What would be your favorite activity at a clan reunion?**

A. The meals
B. Scavenger hunts
C. Three-Pawed race
D. Stories around the fire

QUIZ RESULTS

Mostly As:

You'll do best with some **PRACTICE**. "Practice makes perfect" is true in your case, and the more time you spend working on a problem, the more likely you are to solve it. Just remember not to let the smoke come out of your ears (or snout) if you start to get frustrated. You'll figure it out after a while!

089

Mostly Bs:

Your preferred mode of problem-solving is **DISSECTING**. Sometimes an issue you're facing can seem overwhelming, but if you break it down into smaller, more digestible pieces, you're sure to find the best solution. So take the problem apart, bit by bit, step by step, and use your claws if you have to.

Mostly Cs:

You do well with some **HELP**! Don't be shy; asking another dragon to assist you in your quest will make a world of difference. There's no shame in getting an extra set of paws to lighten your load. And it might make the situation more fun to boot.

Mostly Ds:

You best respond to getting some **DISTANCE**. Does it often feel like you've been trying to figure out a solution to a problem for forever? Take a step back and revisit things in a few hours or even the next day. Time and distance will help. So go for a flight to get your blood pumping, or hit the nest early for a good night's rest. Chances are, by the time you're back at it, you'll have already thought of a good solution.

QUEST

WEATHER THE STORM

POWER UNLOCKED: Perspective
BRAVERY RATING: 🔥🔥

Much like storms, challenges are temporary, even if they don't feel like it in the moment. The key to managing storms is to understand that they can feel overwhelming and all-encompassing, but the dust always settles and the air always clears.

ASK AN **ELDER** DRAGON

What you'll need:
◆ A jar with a lid (an empty and clean jam jar works great)
◆ Glitter or plastic confetti
◆ Waterproof glue
◆ Small toys or decorations

STEP 1: Create a scene at the bottom of your jar using the small toys or decorations. This could be anything from a dragon in a forest to an action figure party to a pattern of holiday baubles. Have fun with it!

STEP 2: Glue these items down. Make sure there's enough room on the sides and above for the glitter or confetti to fall all around them when the time comes. Let the glue dry.

STEP 3: Pour a small amount of the glitter or the confetti into the jar. Keep adding until there is just enough to coat the bottom. (You don't want to add too much, or your scene will be permanently coated in it instead of getting a passing storm.)

STEP 4: Add water until the jar is filled up.

STEP 5: Screw the lid on tight. Shake the jar and see the storm start to whirl, then pass.

NOTE: If your toys or decorations move, don't fret! You can remove the water and glue everything back down.

Make a List, Check It Twice

POWER UNLOCKED: Decisiveness
BRAVERY RATING: 🔥

Dragons are faced with choices all the time, and they can range from giant to itty-bitty. It often helps to make a list of all the things that make you feel zippy about a decision, and the things that make you feel *un*zippy. With enough practice, you'll be able to trust that gut beneath your hide and make the zippiest decision for yourself.

What you'll need:

◆ **A piece of paper**   ◆ **A pen or pencil**

STEP 1: Think of a decision you have to make.

STEP 2: Write down the details of the situation at the top of your piece of paper.

STEP 3: Beneath that, divide the paper into two even sections. Label one section "Zippy" and the other section "Unzippy."

STEP 4: Under the Zippy section, list all of the reasons you can think of that doing the thing at the top of the page would be a good idea.

STEP 5: Under the Unzippy section, list all of the reasons why you *shouldn't* do the thing.

STEP 6: Take a step back to review both sides. Do the zippy reasons outweigh the unzippy ones? Or does it seem like your shiny insides are telling you not to do it?

STEP 7: Think about whether this technique helped you with your choice and if you can use it again in the future!

QUEST

FORTUNE–TELLER

POWER UNLOCKED: Positivity
BRAVERY RATING: 🔥🔥🔥

Remind yourself that good things are on the horizon by thinking about the best version of the future, and all the ways you can get there.

ASK AN **ELDER** DRAGON

What you'll need:
◆ **A piece of paper** ◆ **Scissors** ◆ **A pencil or pen** ◆ **Markers**

STEP 1: Fold the bottom left corner of your piece of paper up to the side of the page. It should form a triangle.

STEP 2: Cut off the top of the piece of paper so that when you unfold it, you're left with a square.

STEP 3: Fold the bottom right corner of your paper to the other side. Unfold it. You should now have crease lines in the shape of an *X*.

STEP 4: Fold each corner toward the center.

STEP 5: Flip the square over. Fold each corner toward the center on this side, too.

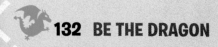

STEP 6: Lift the flaps one by one and write fortunes underneath each triangle that has been formed with your folds (there should be four total).

STEP 7: Refold the flaps and write numbers on the top of each triangle (there should be eight). Flip the square over and use markers to write down the name of a different color on each flap (there should be four total).

STEP 8: Fold the square in half. Slide your thumb and pointer fingers under the flaps. Push your hands together to make the fortune-teller pop up.

STEP 9: Use the fortune-teller to make some predictions. First, pick one of the visible colors and open and close the fortune-teller with your fingers for every letter that spells that color. For example, *r-e-d* would move the fortune-teller three times. Then select one of the four numbers visible. Open and close the fortune-teller that many times. Pick another number and repeat. Then, select a number and read the fortune listed underneath.

You have achieved the first step to a great fortune—dreaming up a wonderful future (and having fun with it in the present)!

Adventure awaits you!

#9
Stick with the dragons that make you glow and help you grow.

FIND YOUR CLAN

Many moons ago, Uwenda the Unique lived in the sprawling Bogte Savannah. Uwenda had many interests that made her feel zippy. She loved a good mystery. She appreciated a piece of dragon fruit. She never felt quite as content as when she gazed up at the quarter moon. The trouble was, Uwenda didn't have anyone with whom she could share all of these wonderful things.

Every year, Uwenda went to the Bogte Full-Moon Festival. She always hoped she'd find a new friend there, so Uwenda made her best dragon-fruit casserole to bring. She reread her favorite mystery so that she could remember all the details to share. She knew when the next quarter moon would arrive and had an easy countdown chart to follow.

When she arrived, Uwenda dropped off her casserole on one of the food tables. Then she made her way to the story booth, where a few dragons were telling a fairy tale. The crowd *oohed* and *aahed* and let out a thunderous applause. "That was great!" she said. "If you like thrilling stories, too, you should try *The Curse of the Old Claw*." The other dragons only smiled politely until the storyteller came back to share another fairy tale. Uwenda's glow began to dim. She thought fairy tales were thrilling, but nothing gave her tail a chill like a good mystery.

Uwenda decided to go get something to eat. She sampled some delicious moon pies and crater cakes. Then she noticed that her dragon-fruit casserole was completely untouched. Uwenda cut off a slice and offered some to the dragon next to her. "No, thank you," the other dragon said. "I'm saving room for some more moon cheese."

Uwenda sighed, realizing that she was different. And different was lonely. Her fur stopped glowing altogether.

The moon dragon left early. She told herself she'd try to lift her spirts in the usual ways—a good story before sleep, some leftover dragon-fruit casserole, painting a quarter moon. She'd find her glow again.

On her way home, Uwenda heard some noise in a distant clearing. She moved to investigate and found it full of other moon dragons gathered round a cozy fire. One of the dragons stood in the center telling ghost stories. Uwenda listened intently. She found herself glowing with happiness.

"Look!" cried the dragon who was telling the story. He was pointing directly at the place where Uwenda was hiding. Startled, Uwenda tried to shrink back into the trees. But her glow was too bright. And she really wanted to hear the rest of the ghost story.

Slowly, Uwenda crept out from the trees and approached the group. "Hi," she said hesitantly. "I'm Uwenda. I was on my way home from the Full-Moon Festival when I heard your story. I love a good mystery."

"Please join us," the storyteller said. And all the other dragons shifted to make room for one more.

"Is that a dragon-fruit casserole?" a young dragon asked, pointing at the tray in Uwenda's claws.

"Dragon fruit is my favorite," the young dragon's grandfather said. "Have you ever tried it grilled with a little bit of sugar?"

Uwenda glowed as the casserole was passed around and everyone took a taste.

"Would you have any interest in meeting us for a viewing of the quarter moon in a few days' time?" the storyteller asked.

"You like the *quarter moon,* too?" Uwenda couldn't believe her good luck. "It's my favorite! I'd love to."

"Hurrah!" the storyteller exclaimed. "I always thought the full moon was a little flashy. We created the Quarter-Moon Society, and we meet monthly in a different spot to enjoy it."

"Join us anytime," squeaked another. "We know we are a bit unique, but we welcome anyone who wants to spend time with us."

Uwenda beamed. Her fur started to glow more brilliantly than ever before. She had never felt so in her element. She wasn't different—she was unique! She'd finally found what she'd been looking for—a few someones who let her be completely herself.

Uwenda joined her quarter-moon clan for every meeting. She began to make up her own mysteries. *The Tell-Tale Tail* became a fan favorite! And she always had a new dragon-fruit recipe to share.

SHINE BRIGHT SO YOUR CLAN CAN FOLLOW YOUR LIGHT.

BUILD A BOND

Finding your clan can feel scary. But remember, these are the dragons that already see you as the very best dragon you can be. They value your sparks and like to share their own. And they make sure you always feel your zippiest.

QUIZ: What's the best bonding activity for your clan, or your ideal clan?

1 **What element do you like best?**

A. Fire
B. Earth
C. Water
D. Air

2 **What is the size of your clan?**

A. Average
B. Huge
C. Pretty small
D. It changes pretty frequently.

3 **What do you have in common with the other members of your clan?**

A. A love of nature
B. An activity or sport
C. Not much but our love for one another
D. A love of relaxation

4 **If your clan were a scent, it would be:**

A. The ocean
B. Grass
C. A feast cooking in the oven
D. Cinnamon

5 **How often do you and your clan get together?**

A. Not often, but it's great when we do.
B. When we're not busy with our own activities
C. All the time; we're always together.
D. Sometimes

6 **Your favorite clan dinner is:**

A. A clambake on the beach
B. Barbecue
C. Takeout
D. A home-cooked meal

7 **Your clan likes to:**

A. Take their time getting up
B. Get up early
C. Everyone has different schedules.
D. Go to bed early

8 **Which snack would be a hit with your clan?**

A. A fruit platter
B. S'mores
C. Sashimi
D. Chips and dip

9 **If there were a crisis, your clan:**

A. Has a disaster kit with all the necessary supplies
B. Has a delegated task for each dragon
C. Has a meeting place
D. All of the above

10 **What's your clan's favorite game to play together?**

A. Marco Polo
B. A tournament of any sort!
C. I Spy
D. Charades

QUIZ RESULTS

Mostly As:

Your clan should go on a **GROUP TRIP**! From a tropical destination to a weekend getaway to a simple afternoon jaunt in a neighboring forest, you and your fellow dragons could do with a break from the day-to-day. You would have a great time taking in a change of scenery and relaxing together.

Mostly Bs:

A **GAME NIGHT** is in order for your clan! Something that bonds you is a shared love of sports or matches. Your favorite family stories might even begin with "and that was the night we invented our own type of dragon chess!" So dust off the paw-ball or the Parcheesi and let the clan building begin!

Mostly Cs:

Your clan likes trying new things, so why not plan a fun **EXCURSION** to mix things up? This could include going to a museum or music festival, or even trying a new type of food. You might start a new clan tradition!

Mostly Ds:

A snug **NIGHT IN** is the perfect activity for your clan. You enjoy putting up your paws after a long day and reconnecting with some wind-down time. The next time you all have a free evening, turn on a favorite movie, grab some hot cocoa, and let the coziness begin!

QUEST
CLAN STUDY

POWER UNLOCKED: Tolerance
BRAVERY RATING: 🔥

Clans come in all shapes and sizes, and can even change over time. Sometimes they're made up of blood relatives, sometimes they're found family. Why not make a record of your current clan?

What you'll need:
◆ **Paper**
◆ **Pens, markers, colored pencils, crayons**

STEP 1: On one side of your paper write down all the things that might make your clan unique. Or, if you're looking for a new clan, write down all the things you'd want to find. See how many different words you can use to describe it.

STEP 2: Flip the piece of paper and draw a portrait of your clan based on what you wrote on the back. Feel free to get creative with it—maybe each member is represented by a colorful glow or with an illustration of their spirit animal.

STEP 3: Hold on to your portrait to share with your fellow dragons at a future date. Or as a guide to finding your ideal clan someday!

INTERVIEW WITH A DRAGON

POWER UNLOCKED: Compassion
BRAVERY RATING: 🔥🔥🔥

There's a lot of wisdom to be gained from listening to another dragon's tales. Sometimes we don't know a lot about the members of our clan, *even* the ones we're closest to.

What you'll need:
◆ A member of your clan
◆ A piece of paper
◆ A pen or pencil
◆ The interview questions on the opposite page

STEP 1: Ask a member of your clan if you can interview them. Set up a good time for both of you.

STEP 2: Start off by thanking your interviewee. Then dive into the questions. Feel free to use the ones below, or create your own questions! Write down their answers on your piece of paper.

① What do the words "clan" or "family" mean to you?

② What are some of your favorite traditions?

③ What is your earliest memory?

④ What is your favorite memory?

⑤ If you could spend one day doing anything, what would you do?

⑥ What is your favorite day of the year?

⑦ Where did you grow up?

⑧ How did you/do you like school?

⑨ What jobs have you had?

⑩ What is your recipe for happiness?

STEP 3: Repeat with as many members of your clan as you'd like!

QUEST

PASS THE FOREST BITES

POWER UNLOCKED: Hospitality
BRAVERY RATING: 🔥🔥🔥🔥🔥

Cooking is a great way to show your clan you care. One key element to any dragon get-together is the food. These bites will keep everyone's energy up during your next shindig.

Forest Bites Recipe

ASK AN
ELDER
DRAGON

What you'll need:

- ◆ 1 cup old-fashioned oats
- ◆ 1/2 cup nut or seed butter (peanut butter, almond butter, sunflower seed butter, etc.—all work)
- ◆ 1/2 cup ground flaxseed
- ◆ 1/3 cup honey or maple syrup
- ◆ Optional: 1/2 cup chopped dates or raisins, 1/2 cup chocolate chips, or 1 tablespoon chia seeds

STEP 1: Mix all of your ingredients together in a bowl.

STEP 2: Roll your batter into bite-size balls and place on a parchment-lined baking sheet or plate.

STEP 3: Refrigerate for 30 to 45 minutes or until set.

STEP 4: Pass around to your clan. These forest bites are good for about a week.

BE THE DRAGON

As your dragon transformation is almost complete, it occurs to me that perhaps there is one last tale to tell. And that tale, my dear friends, is mine.

Well, why did I become a dragon? When I was a young girl, I was not the confident dragon you see before you now. I was shy, a bit on the small side, and I wasn't sure what I had to offer the world. My father was a great knight with battle scars and legends to share. My mother was a princess, brave enough to leave her sheltered castle and see the world. My six siblings all had their talents—math champion, inventor, scientist, longest-jump-roper, trumpet player to the queen, politician. The biggest joys in my life were reading and exploring. If both could be done at the same time, so much the better. But whenever I heard the sound of voices, I would quickly cloak myself and observe.

Sometimes I would spot a group of friends running through the path laughing. I would think, oh, they're having so much fun! But they probably wouldn't want to be friends with the likes of me. I'm too odd and small. Other times, I'd see some sort of argument or even bullying, and I would feel very sad and scared. I'd think, what kind of help would I be?

I became a royal biographer to be close to the action and adventure I longed for, but was too afraid to be part of. But the stories were just that—stories. Fairy tales. Make-believe. It wasn't until I learned about the dragons—until I met the dragons that you've just read about—that I understood.

There is magic to be found if you know where to look— within your clan, in your sparks, and most importantly, in yourself. Be magically, bravely, you.

Be the dragon. The world is full of make-believe. We need more heroes.

TALLYING BRAVERY RATINGS:

Before one last quiz, take a moment to add up the amount of flames you've earned in the quests you've taken so far, and find your results below. Be sure to check in again from time to time to see how your results may change after you embark on more quests or repeat your favorites.

BETWEEN 1 AND 20 FLAMES: *Great! Your roar has some real gusto behind it, and your hide is starting to glimmer. You will be flying about in no time.*

BETWEEN 20 AND 40 FLAMES: *Well done! You have discovered the treasure within yourself and in other creatures. Guard it at all costs!*

BETWEEN 40 AND 50 FLAMES: *Excellent! You have taken the art of helping others to new heights. You are well on your way to becoming a legendary dragon hero.*

ABOVE 50 FLAMES: *Hurrah! You are a fearless leader, ready to help all dragon-kind. Of course, the wisest dragon knows there are always more powers to unlock, so this is really only the beginning!*

BE YOUR OWN HERO

There are many kinds of heroes. New quests and experiences will change your perspective over time, too. Be sure to come back to all of the quizzes and quests in this book to see how you've grown.

QUIZ: What type of dragon hero are you right now?

1 What are you most drawn to?

A. Clouds
B. Sand
C. Stardust
D. Dirt

2 When faced with a problem, you:

A. Take care to solve it on your own
B. Try a few different things to figure it out
C. Look to your loved ones for advice
D. Look at both sides of the issue before finding the right answer

3 You've been called:

A. Courageous
B. Talented
C. Sweet
D. Curious

4 You always appreciate a:

A. Great conversation
B. Workout that gets the blood pumping
C. Piece of cake
D. Bubble bath

5 **When getting somewhere, you'd rather:**

A. Soar

B. Run quickly

C. Frolic

D. Swim

6 **What's the ideal forecast?**

A. A snowy evening

B. A hot afternoon

C. A cool night

D. A slight breeze

7 **When invited to a party, you bring the:**

A. Music

B. Board games

C. Food

D. Candles

8 **Your favorite part of a hike is the:**

A. Roaring while climbing uphill

B. Opportunity for hide-and-seek

C. Chatting with your fellow hikers

D. Quiet time

9 **What type of music best represents you?**

A. Soul

B. Rock

C. Pop

D. Oldies

10 **If you could live anywhere, it would be:**

A. On a seaside cliff

B. In the desert

C. Near plains

D. Next to a forest

QUIZ RESULTS

Mostly As:

You are a hero who uses your **VOICE**. Whether it's roaring to enhance your courage or sticking up for those who feel silenced, you have a strong sense of what's right. Your bravery knows no bounds and you pride yourself in getting things done—even when they're hard or seem scary. You also have many hidden talents and love to travel.

Mostly Bs:

You are a hero who uses your **PASSION**. There's a fire brewing in that belly of yours, and it fuels your hard work and determination. Your generous attitude and limitless energy are contagious to those around you, and you also know the power in asking for help. You feel quite at home in the great outdoors and do what you can to protect Mother Earth.

Mostly Cs:

You are a hero who uses your **COMPASSION**. Your heart tends to sense what others are feeling beneath their hides, which is a magic of its own. You genuinely care about those around you and often use your creativity to connect with them. You understand the value of being different and appreciate a good adventure as well as a good story.

Mostly Ds:

You are a hero who uses your **WISDOM**. You are smart and good at problem-solving. You also know that you still have much to learn, which makes you very special. You garner the respect of the dragons around you and always follow your dreams, however out of reach they may seem. You love to relax with a nice bath or a mug of warm milk after a long day of thinking.

Catherine J. Manning is a children's book writer and editor in Los Angeles. She lives with her husband, her son, and her sassy cat.

Melanie Demmer is an American artist born and raised in Plymouth, Michigan. She has been drawing since she was a little girl. Back then, her favorite canvas was pavement and her go-to tool was sidewalk chalk. Nowadays, Melanie typically works digitally but also enjoys creating artwork with watercolor, markers, colored pencils, and acrylic paint. Oh, and sometimes a pinch of glitter, too! Melanie now resides in Salt Lake City, Utah. To find out more, follow her on Instagram @melaniedemmer.